BANGOR

THEN AND NOW

—————— A Pictorial Record ——————

Published 2012 by
Colourpoint Creative Ltd
Colourpoint House, Jubilee Business Park
Jubilee Road, Newtownards, BT23 4YH
Tel: 028 9182 6339
Fax: 028 9182 1900
E-mail: info@colourpoint.co.uk
Web: www.colourpoint.co.uk

First Edition
First Impression

Designed by April Sky Design, Newtownards
Tel: 028 9182 7195
Web: www.aprilsky.co.uk

Printed by GPS Colour Graphics, Belfast

ISBN 978-1-78073-045-5

Front cover: The Long Hole, Then and Now. Two images, taken over a century apart, brought together as one.
Inshore fishing boats, rowing boats and a two masted schooner, probably photographed in the last years of the
nineteenth century (p96), combined with Seacliff Road's pastel coloured terraces as pictured in 2012 (p97).

Rear cover: Queen's Parade, as photographed in 1936 by Valentine & Sons Ltd.

Explore, discover and buy other titles on Northern Ireland
subjects at BooksNI.com – the online bookshop for Northern Ireland

BANGOR

THEN AND NOW

A Pictorial Record

Adam G Bell

COLOURPOINT BOOKS

Queen's Parade, Then and Now. The upper portion of this image is taken from a postcard view which dates to the late 1930s. Establishments such as the Locarno Restaurant and Fish Buffet (famous for its delicious chips, said to have been the best in the town), Caproni's Café (equally famous for its ice cream and advertised at the time as "The largest confectionery establishment in Bangor"), the Regent Palace Hotel (which in 1938 boasted of its "splendid ballroom" and "dining accommodation for 600") and the Arcadia (an amusement outlet operated by Barry's, featuring slot machines, variety concerts, 'Snow Freeze' ice cream and a palmist called Madame Sarosa) all catered to the thousands of holidaymakers who annually descended upon Bangor. Photographer (lower): Alan Hartley

To my grandparents

Margaret and Gary Graham
Jean and Billy Bell

Introduction

It was at a market in Blackrock, on the outskirts of Dublin, that I came across my first old postcard of Bangor. A sepia tone view of Ward Park showing the rustic pergola and war memorial, the postcard had been sent in 1937 to Mrs Saunders at 1 Sydenham Place, Dundrum, Co Dublin. The message read, "Thursday. Just a line to let you know how I am getting along. Weather has improved wonderfully, but at night it is cold enough. I hope you are minding yourself. I was very glad to hear you had some heating. How are all the doggies, I saw about 7 pekes, one black, all together near Bangor yesterday. I also saw the Bros. Justice at Bangor, I think they take a house here for Sept. Will let you know def time I arrive on Mon. Best love, Elsie".

Delighted at the unexpected novelty of coming across something from my hometown, I snapped up the postcard. One of the first things I did upon returning to Bangor was to bring my new acquisition with me to Ward Park and, standing in the same spot as the original photographer, I attempted to recreate the image. Two decades and over 800 postcards later, my interest in the history of my hometown and its changing face led me to join forces with Bangor & North Down Camera Club in the production of this book.

Picture postcards were first introduced to the British Isles in 1894. The following decade saw an explosion in sales and the early years of the new century came to be known as the Golden Age of the Postcard, when an estimated six billion cards were sent in the UK – the equivalent of 200 cards per person!

With six or more deliveries a day in urban areas, postcards were incredibly popular as a cheap and reliable means of communication. Moreover, as attractive items in their own right, Edwardian ladies in particular took to collecting picture postcards in large numbers, and the survival of their treasured postcard albums has ensured that many interesting examples remain today. Although the market for postcards was reduced after the First World War with the spread of the telephone, picture postcards remained popular among holidaymakers as a means of communicating with family and friends 'back home'.

The scenes depicted on old postcards provide a fascinating window on the past, but for me the appeal of postcard collecting is as much about discovering the messages penned by the senders, as enjoying the views on the front. Some messages are short and sweet – the sender of one card in 1913 simply wrote "Hallo!" – while the extent of another correspondent's message in 1908 was to admit, "I'm quite stuck for something to say". Writing in 1940 to Mrs McIlveen at 48 Westland Street, Shankill Road, Belfast, 'Tommy' summed up his time in Bangor in just five words, declaring that he "Could stick it for life". Occasionally senders make apology for a lengthy interval since their last communication, such as Captain W Tait who, in his postcard to Miss B Richardson of Strathdon, Aberdeenshire, wrote in August 1916, "Dear Bessie. Just a P.C. to let you know I am still in the land of the living".

The weather is, predictably, a common topic of conversation. In 1912 Ellie wrote to Miss M Robinson at 47 Sandy Row, Belfast, "Having a great time here, I have a lovely sunburn of face" while another correspondent boasted in 1903 of the "dandy weather" and "how brown I am getting". At the other end of the spectrum, one visitor was confined to his Prospect Road boarding house in September 1903 because it "simply poured all day" and in 1957 'Ann' wrote, "Managing to enjoy ourselves in spite of the lousy weather". In 1939 an optimistic soul wrote to Mr JT Murray of Consett,

Co Durham, that "It was windy yesterday & is raining heavily to-day, but we are hoping for improvement". Ironically, the image on Mr Murray's card shows sun-kissed holidaymakers dozing on deckchairs at Marine Gardens!

Then as now, being on holiday can be an opportunity to relax and let others take care of life's chores. Writing to her son George in 1920, one Manchester woman declared, "The woman cooks for us, we have nothing to do but dress & go out". Perhaps the sender of the card to a Miss Whyte of Fraserburgh, Aberdeenshire, in 1910, took a certain delight in asking her correspondent, "I hope you are progressing with your spring clean?" and in 1974 'Lorraine' urged her colleagues at County Hall, Ballymena, "Don't work too hard (ha ha)".

Aside from the usual commentary on the weather, accommodation and holiday amusements, I have also come across some very unexpected messages. One postcard, sent in 1909 to Miss N Brown of 16 Rose Street, Wokingham, Berkshire, starts off with "I had a lovely journey across. The water was as smooth as a lake …" Things, however, go downhill for the author from hereon in. He continues "… but we ran into 3 fogs & arrived at Belfast at 9.30 instead of 6 o'clock. My tooth bled the whole night & I had to remain on deck. This morning I went to the chemist. He doctored it & I had to lie on my back 4 hours. He had to plug it. An artery was cut". Discovering messages like this makes the pursuit of postcard collecting all the more interesting. One wonders what poor Miss Brown's reaction was upon reading that! Many of the postcards featured in this book are accompanied by intriguing messages, I hope you will enjoy discovering them as much as I did.

Adam G Bell
September 2012

Clandeboye House

Clandeboye, Co. Down

Posted 24 September 1917
Publisher: Valentine, Dublin

The Blackwood family came to North Down from Scotland in the early seventeenth century, setting up home at Clandeboye. Ballyleidy House, as it was then known, was built for James Blackwood, 2nd Baron Dufferin, in 1804. The 5th Baron, Frederick Hamilton-Temple-Blackwood, later 1st Marquess of Dufferin & Ava, was its most celebrated owner. Remembered as a gifted diplomat, Lord Dufferin served as Governor General of Canada (1872–1879), Ambassador to Russia (1879–1881) and to the Ottoman Empire (1881–1884), Viceroy of India (1884–1888), Ambassador to Italy (1888–1891) and to France (1891–1896). The 1st Marquess filled Clandeboye with curios and treasures from far-flung lands, and the bedrooms were named after places connected with his career, such as St Petersburg, Simla and Rome. Sent to JW Chapple of Leamington Spa, the message on this postcard reads, "Dear Mr Chapple. Arrived safely. Hope you're not lonely. This is a view of Dufferin's estate where I got my training. Yours, J Gore". It would seem the sender was one of the many young men who, as part of the 36th (Ulster) Division, received their training at Clandeboye, before serving on the Western Front.

The vista across the shamrock-shaped lake created by the 1st Marquess is today an enduring legacy of Lord Dufferin's romantic remodelling of the lands surrounding his family seat, a process embarked upon after attaining his majority in 1847. We are also reminded of Dufferin's role as a landlord during the famine years of the 1840s, when he reduced his tenants' rents and set up relief projects, one of which saw the creation of this lake. Today, Clandeboye is home to the Marchioness of Dufferin & Ava, wife of the late 5th Marquess Sheridan, and is one of the few great estates of Ireland still owned by the original family. It boasts the largest area of broadleaved woodland in Northern Ireland, in addition to 250 hectares of farmland. Award winning Holstein and Jersey cows are bred on the estate and, since 2007, their milk has been used to produce a range of luxury yoghurt.

Helen's Tower

BANGOR. - HELEN'S TOWER.

Standing at the top of a hill about a mile from Clandeboye House is Helen's Tower. Built by the 1st Marquess between 1848 and 1850, Helen's Tower was a devoted son's monument to his adoring mother. Helen Selina Sheridan, Baroness Dufferin and subsequently Countess of Gifford, encouraged her son in a love of the arts and championed his rise in society. Dufferin asked leading poets of the day to pen poems in his mother's honour, which were then engraved on brass panels and installed in the tower. Alfred, Lord Tennyson, opened his poem with the lines:

> Helen's Tower here I stand,
> Dominant over sea and land.
> Son's love built me, and I hold
> Mother's love in lettered gold.

Addressed to Mrs Strachan at 17 Hamilton Road, Bangor, the sender simply wrote, "In town to-day", surely the equivalent of a modern day text message!

Posted 14 December 1914
Publisher: G Lowden & Co, Bangor

Today the Irish Landmark Trust is the custodian of Helen's Tower, which has recently been restored and is enjoying a new lease of life as a unique self catering holiday home, one of 19 historic buildings restored by the Trust throughout Ireland since 1992. A replica of Helen's Tower was erected in 1921 at Thiepval in northern France, dedicated to the men of the 36th (Ulster) Division, which suffered heavy losses on the first day of the Battle of the Somme. Helen's Tower was chosen as the inspiration for the memorial because the Ulster Division were camped at Clandeboye, within sight of Helen's Tower, before being sent to the battlefields of France and Belgium.

Photographer:
Shirley Graham

Church Street and Bangor Abbey

OLD BANGOR.

Posted 15 December 1914
Publisher: G Lowden & Co, Bangor

Church Street was part of Church Quarter, an ancient part of the town called after the Abbey Church, seen here in the distance. Aged residents of Church Quarter are said to have called Church Street 'Fourth Row' or 'Four Raw' in mid Victorian times, which could have been derived from 'Fort Row', in reference to an earth fort which may have once surrounded the Abbey. In this view Church Street is mainly composed of whitewashed single storey weavers' cottages. Sexton and grave digger Dan McKeown operated four looms. He had a "little black dog which sat at the corner of the house and yelped at the time the church bell was ringing". Church Street was also known for its eccentric characters, chief of which was the barefooted Sammy Reavey, who had a habit of walking backwards and was never without his trademark tall hat, inside which he was known to keep coal, beef, bones, bread and carrots! Then there was David Ferguson, who determined to leave his wife and book a passage to Australia after discovering that she indulged in snuff. "A woman who would snuff would drink", insisted David, "and them that would drink would do something worse".

Although the whitewashed cottages have long since disappeared, Bangor Abbey provides a continuity with the days of old Church Quarter. The tower is the oldest part of the Abbey, dating back to the fifteenth century, to which the octagonal spire was added in 1693. The site, however, was once home to a celebrated monastic settlement of almost 3,000 monks, founded by St Comgall in AD 558. From Bangor, monks such as St Columbanus and St Gall travelled across Europe, founding important monasteries and spreading Christianity. Bangor's rapid growth in the late nineteenth century led to the closure of the Abbey in 1882 in favour of the newly built Parish Church of St Comgall, which was larger and more conveniently sited. But the town's growth continued apace, and in 1917 the mothballed Abbey was brought back into service again as a place of worship. A stroll around the churchyard reveals many fine eighteenth and nineteenth century headstones, including that to Captain George Colville who "dauntless trod ye fluctuating sea" and went down with his ship, the *Amazon,* at Ballyholme in 1780.

St Comgall's Roman Catholic Church, Brunswick Road

No. 16   R.C. CHURCH, BRUNSWICK ROAD, BANGOR, CO. DOWN.

Unposted, about 1910
Publisher: Hurst & Co, Belfast

Originally called the Ash Loanen, Brunswick Road was little more than a lane through open countryside when the first chapel was built in 1851, seen here on the left. Before its erection, mass had been celebrated in an "empty house in Ballymagee Street [High Street], which at other times was used for itinerant shows". As the Catholic population grew, there was an ever increasing need for a new church, and in 1890 the original chapel was replaced by the fine Gothic Revival church, seen on the right of this image. Rev Patrick McConvey, Parish Priest of Newtownards, was responsible for its building and he travelled from Newtownards each morning after Mass, standing over the workmen like a foreman! 1916 saw the arrival of the gifted Rev Patrick Scally as Parish Priest of Bangor, who soon raised the funds to install stained glass windows, a marble pulpit, a mosaic pavement in the Sanctuary and the Stations of the Cross. After building the Little Flower Hall in 1926, Fr Scally turned his attention to the building of a new school and St Comgall's was opened in 1929. It was also Fr Scally who was responsible for introducing a religious order of nuns to Bangor in 1932.

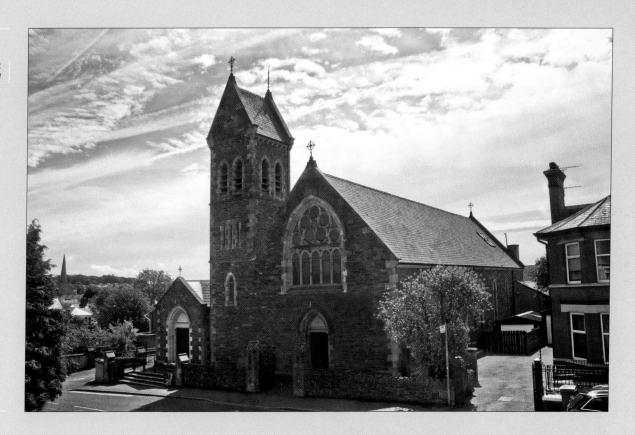

The original chapel of 1851, popularly known as the 'Old Building', was converted into a mixed boys' and girls' school upon the arrival of Rev Peter McKenna in 1890, a function it continued to serve until St Comgall's Primary School was built in 1929. The Old Building was eventually demolished in 1984. In the late 1960s and early 1970s the Little Flower Hall was transformed each Friday night into the fondly remembered 'Coffin Disco' where the DJ would "climb out of a spot lit coffin" at the start of the night. Claire Gray recalls that "It was an excellent disco attended by young people from across the town", adding that "The Priest used to patrol outside"!

Bangor Castle

BANGOR CASTLE, CO. DOWN.

Posted 25 July 1905
Publisher: Frederick Hartmann

Bangor Castle is at least the third mansion house on this site, the first being a "fayre stone house" built by the Scotsman Sir James Hamilton soon after he was granted large tracts of land by James I in 1605. In 1709 Anne Hamilton, heiress of the Bangor lands, married Michael Ward of Castle Ward, Co Down, and in 1852 the Hon Robert Edward Ward built the present Bangor Castle. A substantial landowner, pre-eminent member of the Corporation and, from 1864, an elected Town Commissioner, RE Ward was an influential figure in Bangor at a time of great change, who involved himself with many developments in education, healthcare, church and harbour provision. Sent to Miss E Salkeld of Whitley Bay, Northumberland, the message on this card reads, "11 Alfred Street, Bangor. Dear Ethel, I have been enjoying myself grand, bathing & cycling. I do hope you are better. I will write when we go home. Many thanks for p.c. Best love, from Annie".

Photographer:
Gerry Coe

In 1878 RE Ward's only child Maude married John Bingham, 5th Baron Clanmorris from Co Mayo, and they made Bangor Castle their home. Lord and Lady Clanmorris had ten children, including Barry Bingham, who was awarded the Victoria Cross for his actions in engaging the German fleet at the Battle of Jutland in 1916. Following the death of Lady Clanmorris in February 1941, the Castle and parkland were sold to Bangor Borough Council. Much of the demesne became Castle Park, and the Castle itself was converted for use as the Town Hall in 1952. The Great Hall or Music Room where RE Ward "indulged his passion for organ music in medieval splendour" now serves as the Council chamber. In 1984 the outbuildings were adapted to create North Down Heritage Centre, now North Down Museum.

Castle Park

Castle Park, Bangor, Co. Down.   RT.227

Posted 1974–1975
Publisher: Valentine & Sons Ltd

Castle Park was opened to the public in 1945 by the Governor of Northern Ireland William Leveson-Gower, 4th Earl Granville. The Park, formerly the demesne of Bangor Castle, was originally enclosed by a high wall, the stones of which were said to have been quarried at the Long Hole. Although private land until the 1940s, visitors were admitted from time to time, as indicated by WG Lyttle in his guide to the 'Bangor Season' in 1885, which states that the Castle grounds were open every Saturday and were "well worthy of inspection". During the Second World War the Castle and parkland were used by the military, and Nissen huts erected in the grounds. Following the war, Castle Park was the setting for many entertainments including horse and cattle shows, sheep dog trials (including the Irish National Championships), motorcycle racing, fireworks displays and open air circuses.

Photographer:
Gerry Coe

Seen from the north front of the Castle, the ornamental rose garden, complete with shamrock-shaped flower beds, remains an attractive feature of Castle Park to this day. In the foreground at centre is a carved stone chapiter "brought from Africa by James Hamilton Ward, Admiral". A stroll in the woods surrounding the Castle reveals a fine collection of trees, with specimens from as far afield as the Andes, the Rocky Mountains, the Himalayas and Japan. Also to be found in the shade of this quiet wooded setting is the burial plot of the Clanmorris family, last occupants of Bangor Castle. Since 2009 the once neglected walled garden adjoining the Valentine playing fields has been brought back to life as a haven of horticultural tranquillity, complete with a fountain and lovingly tended flowerbeds.

Bangor Castle from Upper Main Street

BANGOR CASTLE & PARK, BANGOR, Co. DOWN.

Posted 5 June 1964
Publisher: ETW Dennis & Sons Ltd

Bangor Castle, seen in the distance at centre, is viewed here from the southern end of Upper Main Street. The Castle, along with 148 acres of parkland, was purchased by Bangor Borough Council in November 1941 for £34,000. The cost of acquiring the Castle was offset by selling a portion of the parkland where, during the 1960s and 1970s, a new police station, leisure centre, schools, nurses' homes and a technical college were built. Sent to Miss J Rowley of Hull, the message reads, "Have been here for about a week and had a very enjoyable time with lots of coach tours. Apart from some rain showers, and at nights, a keen coldness, we have enjoyed our stay but go back tomorrow evening to Stranraer and a week in Ayr. Regards to all of you at no. 51, from Cathy & Allan".

Photographer:
Harry Watson

Although the card opposite was posted in June 1964, the new police station which opened two years earlier is not visible. Records kept by the postcard publishers indicate that the view was in fact taken in 1957. When the police moved to Castle Park Avenue from their old base in Victoria Road, the *County Down Spectator* described the new surroundings as "well-lighted, cheerfully decorated and most congenial". The delayed creation of the car park in the middle distance is a lesson for those who neglect to read the small print. In the mid 1920s Bangor Urban District Council acquired this portion of the Castle demesne with the intention of widening Abbey Street and creating a car park. When work commenced on the car park the Council received a letter pointing out that the lease contained a clause that no cars could be parked within 40 feet of the demesne wall! Frustrated Council officials were forced to postpone plans for a car park on the site until after the purchase of the Castle and parkland in 1941.

Bangor Railway Station

BANGOR STATION.

Posted 25 July 1923
Publisher: WA Green, Belfast

In 1862 RE Ward of Bangor Castle cut the first sod for the Belfast, Holywood & Bangor Railway Company's extension of the line from Holywood to Bangor. The terminus, an Italianate design in polychrome brickwork, was built on the site of a market garden owned by Hamilton Halliday. The fruit trees which had grown there were carted to another of Mr Halliday's market gardens at Sydenham. By May 1865, the first railway passengers were arriving at Bangor, signalling the start of a prosperous new era for the town. The station master's house stood below the station on Abbey Street. William Smith, the first station master, eventually "got religious and thought it was not right to work on Sunday, so he gave in his notice and left". The sender of this card wrote to Mrs Dunlop at Bann Road, Dromore, "I am having a lovely time in Bangor. Just back from having a run to Donaghadee". The photographer, WA Green, has captured a busy scene, including five young women strolling arm in arm, and a little girl clutching a wooden spade, in anxious anticipation of Bangor's sandy shores.

Photographer:
Jack Thompson

The second half of the twentieth century saw substantial alterations to the original station building. By the 1990s Bangor railway station was a shadow of its former self, the elegant brick façade by now plastered over and clad in corrugated metal. Writing in 1999, Marcus Patton said of the once grand terminus, "If a competition was ever held for the most unrecognisable building by Charles Lanyon, this would surely win it". A new station building was badly needed, and Newcastle upon Tyne architects, The Napper Partnership, were awarded the commission. Their brief: to design a "state of the art, user-friendly transport centre". The new combined bus and railway station was officially opened in April 2001. It makes dramatic use of glass and steel in a nautically inspired design, the chief feature of which is the curved 'wave' profile of the undulating roof canopy. The public waiting areas were enlarged threefold, providing 750 square metres of public space, at the centre of which is a bright double-height concourse.

Upper Main Street from the Railway Station forecourt

Posted 9 March 1974
Publisher: NPO
Photographer: TR McIlroy

Prominent in this image is the new post office, opened in 1936. Built in the neoclassical style so often favoured for civic buildings of the 1930s, it is one of only two post offices and a handful of telephone exchanges in the United Kingdom to bear the cypher of Edward VIII, who acceded the throne on 20 January 1936, only to abdicate later that year on 11 December. Skirting the roundabout in the foreground are a couple of Austins and a Jaguar. Sent to Mr & Mrs V Atwater of Lyndale, London NW2 in March 1974, the message reads, "Just a few words to let you know that I've arrived home safely – no hijacking! The weather here is surprisingly good and my family are all in reasonably good shape. Many thanks for your hospitality. Shall write a letter later. Love, Anne".

Photographer:
Adam Bell

The 'new' post office of 1936 remains in its dominant position on the corner of Upper Main Street and Castle Park Avenue, however, the Mark 1 Jaguar has been replaced by an indigo blue X-Type and its companions in front and behind are a Suzuki and a Hyundai. The terrace to the left of the post office replaced much older two storey dwellings in the first few years of the twentieth century. It was in this area in March 1993 that a car bomb caused extensive damage to property and four police officers were injured. Returning to the message penned by Anne in the postcard opposite, seeking to reassure her London hosts that her return to Northern Ireland was not marred by terrorist activity, we are reminded that while Bangor escaped much of the sectarian violence of the Troubles, the threat was never very far away, and could sometimes be all too real.

Dufferin Avenue

DUFFERIN AVENUE, BANGOR.

Posted 5 July 1923
*Publisher: Eason & Son Ltd,
Dublin & Belfast*

Dufferin Avenue was named after the 1st Marquess of Dufferin & Ava. The part shown here, from Southwell Road to the junction with Princetown Road, was developed in the last decade of the nineteenth century, up until which point it had been fields farmed by Captain McCullough of Rathgael. The houses visible at far left are part of Inkerman Terrace, named after their builder, Captain Inkerman Brown. Born in 1857, Captain Brown was himself named after the Crimean War battle of 1854, in which an uncle had been killed. The rents from Inkerman Terrace were intended to provide security for Captain Brown's family, should anything happen to him. Events proved his foresight, as the Captain and his entire crew were lost at sea when his ship the *Antrim* went down with all hands on 2 April 1902 en route from Newport, South Wales, to Belfast. Sent to C Wilkinson at 198 Agnes Street, off Belfast's Shankill Road, the sender was "Having a lovely time here".

The section of road falling steeply from Upper Main Street to Southwell Road, directly behind the photographer, is the oldest part of Dufferin Avenue. Known separately as Catherine Place until its incorporation with Dufferin Avenue at around the turn of the last century, the terrace on the north side dates to about 1840 and was considered "the swell street in Bangor" in the mid nineteenth century. The three storey terrace curving into Southwell Road, at right, is Landerville Crescent. Until about 1850 an open stream ran above ground along Southwell Road to the sea. Southwell Road takes its name from an ancient sulphur well which was located between Central Avenue and Primrose Street, possibly near the foot of King Street. The well, now built over, was said to have healing properties, probably stemming from a legend that St Comgall cured a monk's blindness by application of its water.

Upper Main Street looking south west

Posted 19 November 1908
Publisher: Valentine, Dublin
Retailer: William Dunn, 26, 28
& 30 Main Street, Bangor

The girl at far left is standing outside what was then the post office, complete with Postmaster's house above. Joe Breen was Postmaster at the time. His daughter, Muriel Breen, later recalled the operation of the post office in her childhood, "Bicycles were used intensively and I remember hand carts for despatching and receiving mailbags from the train to and from Belfast. They always arrived at the last minute and were preceded by shouts of "Make way for the Royal Mail". It was a phrase with which I was very familiar and sounded so important". Sent to Miss Rowland of Yeovil, Somerset, the author of this postcard advises the recipient that she has heard from Randolph, who has "gone to the States after all". Between 1851 and 1921 2.5 million people emigrated from Ireland. For the vast majority, America was the preferred destination.

Photographer:
Jack Thompson

The imposing demesne wall of Bangor Castle, seen running along the left hand side of Abbey Street in the view opposite, was removed by the Council after the Second World War. Hidden from view in both images, at the end of the terrace at right, is the Ava bar, which was built as a doctor's house about 1840. Now sadly removed but visible in the earlier view is the male lime tree which grew in front of the Ava for well over a century. Built in the late 1990s, the Menarys complex replaced what had been Robinson & Cleaver's in the 1970s. Also here was the original premises of the *County Down Spectator*, founded in 1904, which occupied the three storey building with the pair of castellated bow oriel windows, seen in the postcard view.

Upper Main Street looking north east

Upper Main Street, **Bangor.**

Posted 1912–1918
*Publisher: Eason & Son Ltd,
Dublin & Belfast*

The two storey building opposite the horse and cart was built in 1867 as the manse of First Bangor Presbyterian Church, and was used as such until about 1912. In this view, the presence of awnings reveals that it was now occupied by shopkeepers, including jeweller and silversmith William Pollock at no 104. Closer to the photographer, the building with the street lamp in front would later become J & R Mayne's garage, complete with petrol pumps on the edge of the pavement. For the time being, however, the motor car was still a rare sight, there being only about 1,000 cars spread throughout the north of Ireland by 1914. The sender of this card writes to his young nieces in Derby, "Dear Little girls, it is raining ever so hard & uncle is having to stay in. He may go on to Portrush on Monday but doesn't know yet. Give uncle's love to mother and daddy, please. Love from uncle Geo".

In 1912 William Pollock placed an advertisement in the *County Down Spectator* informing "residents and visitors" that it was no longer necessary to look beyond Bangor for "a nice piece of jewellery or silver plate, watches, clocks, spoons, forks, knives, &c", insisting that he would give "better value than you can get in Belfast". Readers were encouraged to call and inspect Pollock's stock, with the added assurance that no one would be "importuned to buy". To the right of Pollock's at no 102 was Gibson "The Drapery Specialist" who, in 1912, advertised their new line of blouses as possessing a "daintiness of design and a freshness of treatment", while ironmonger James McMullan at no 108 announced that his seasonable stock included crocks for preserving eggs, meat safes, pea trainers, garden hose and lawn tennis balls. Nos 102–112 Main Street were rebuilt about 1975 and modernised again in recent years, following the construction of the Menary's complex to the south.

Upper Main Street looking towards the Ward Schools

Posted 17 December 1912
Publisher: William Ritchie & Sons Ltd

The little dog in the bottom left corner is my favourite part of this wonderful image. Follow the sightline of the dog and you come to a three storey building with an awning, which was used around the turn of the century as tea rooms and, from 1911, reading and recreation rooms. Its neighbour, complete with a fine cupola, was then the Ward Male, Female and Infant National Schools. The principals were husband and wife, William and Anne McDonagh. Mrs McDonagh, remembered Muriel Breen, "inspected everybody's hands and nails at least once a week and taught sewing very unsympathetically". Before becoming a school, this fine building had been erected about 1820 as the town's Court House and Market House. The building with the pink striped awning was Simon's, a ladies and gents outfitter, remembered for its old fashioned system of conveying money in carriers from the counter to the cash office and back again. The three storey, four bay building to its left was JS Balmer's chemist.

Photographer:
Adam Bell

Although many of the buildings pictured opposite have been swept away, the scene is recognisable today thanks to the survival of the old Market House, now Northern Bank. Records from the early 1860s show that the Church Education Society had a school room in this building, and following a refurbishment of the facilities in 1885, paid for by RE Ward, the schools were renamed in their patron's honour. The Ward Schools occupied the building until 1933, when it became the Town Hall. In 1952 the Belfast Banking Co moved in when the Town Hall relocated to Bangor Castle, and the cupola was removed.

The reading and recreation rooms to its left were replaced in 1920 by the present Ulster Bank, the upper floors of which originally incorporated a house for the bank manager. Mostly dating from the 1890s, the buildings to the right of the Ward Schools in the image opposite have all since been demolished. The building now occupied by Boots, on the corner of Main Street and Castle Street, was built in 1982. It replaced an earlier building which, for many years, was the site of Warden's newsagents. This area is still known among older Bangor residents as 'Warden's Corner'.

First Bangor Presbyterian Church, Upper Main Street

BANGOR PRESBYTERIAN CHURCH.

Presbyterianism in Bangor has its origins in the early seventeenth century when the Rev Robert Blair moved to the town from Ayrshire, at the invitation of his patron Sir James Hamilton. The congregation first worshipped at Fisher Hill (Victoria Road) and by the mid eighteenth century had relocated to a building on the corner of Ballymagee Street (High Street) and Quay Street, where they remained until the present church was completed in 1834. In the 1830s the parish of Bangor was composed of 9,355 souls, of which 8,230 were Presbyterians. A reminder of a time when farming was a more prominent feature in the town, the message on this postcard, addressed to Mrs Hugh Scott of Craigtarra, Annadale Avenue, Ballynafeigh, reads, "Kingscourt, Bangor. Dear Aunt. Sorry I can't accept your kind invitation for to-day, owing to getting hay cut, but would be pleased if uncle & you would come down to see us some day this week. Bangor is looking lovely at present. With love to all, yours sincerely, Annie".

Posted about 1910
Publisher: The National Series

Although the postcard opposite was not franked, it dates to around 1910. John Waddell, who in 1937 became Moderator of the Irish Presbyterian Church, was minister at First Bangor from 1902 to 1914. It is said that his departure was hastened by his objection to the signing of the Ulster Covenant on church premises in 1912. The tower and slender white spire, added to mark the church's golden jubilee in 1881, provide a contrast with the basalt construction of its main body. The weeping ash in front of the portico has witnessed over a century and a half of change. In the early 1920s a suggestion was made to erect a life-size statue of a soldier, in memory of the town's war dead, in place of the tree, which was reckoned to be "dying and … would have to come away in any case". After much debate, a memorial was instead erected in Ward Park, and the old tree is still going strong today!

Photographer:
Adam Bell

Upper Main Street looking from the crest of the hill

No. 17   MAIN STREET, BANGOR, CO. DOWN.

Posted 5 July 1917
Publisher: Hurst & Co, Belfast

In this splendid view we see the full stretch of Upper Main Street, busy with townspeople and visitors. The awnings along the left hand side shade most of the shop fronts from the afternoon sun, which is casting long shadows over the opposite side of the street. Apart from horses and carts, a bicycle is the only other form of transport visible. A cast iron water trough stood just round the corner, outside the railings of the Parish Church, providing a welcome drink for horses on just such a summer's day. We get a good view in this postcard of David Warden's newsagents, the gable end of which sports a pair of large enamel signs advertising 'Van Houten's Cocoa'. David's son James took over the business in the mid 1920s and by the 1940s his shop had moved round the corner to no 4 Castle Street. In her message to Miss A Martin of Magheral, Katesbridge, the sender apologises for "not writing to you long ago … I have just got the chance now of sending you this PC to let you know I am still alive & in Bangor".

In her autobiography *Liquorice All-Sorts*, Muriel Breen recalled Warden's as, "one of those old fashioned shops with two large crammed windows – the whole shop was cluttered with papers and things. 'Jeemes', as everybody called the owner, never got rid of a single paper, except what he sold. It was almost impossible to get inside, as there was only a single gangway. Yet he had everything necessary in the way of stationery and always knew where things were. It wouldn't

be allowed nowadays, as it was a fire hazard. 'Jeemes' himself was tall and thin and beaky and his clothes hung on him. His tweed hat came down to his nose, which always had a drop at the end." Legend has it that when Jimmy Warden died, hundreds of pound notes were discovered scattered amongst the piles of old newspapers which he had hoarded!

Hamilton Road

HAMILTON ROAD, BANGOR, CO. DOWN.

Unposted, about 1910
*Publisher: James Conolly,
Scrabo House, Bangor*

In the foreground at right is the Parish Church of St Comgall, consecrated in 1882. When the belfry and spire were completed 17 years later, 76 year old Rector of St Comgall's Dean Edward Maguire was hoisted in a builder's cage to bless the topmost stone. A bell which had belonged to an old church at Clandeboye, formerly "swung on the fork of a tree", was rung in the new Parish Church until it received its present peal of eight bells in 1899. Beyond St Comgall's is the ornately decorated Masonic Hall, built about 1880, and to its left is the Dufferin Memorial Hall of 1905, erected in memory of the distinguished 1st Marquess of Dufferin & Ava (1826–1902). Although built as a parish hall, for some decades after its completion it was considered "the cultural and social centre of Bangor", where packed audiences enjoyed performances by Bangor Operatic Society and Bangor Drama Club. It was also where Glenlola and other school prize distributions took place, as well as being a venue for political meetings and ballet classes! Bookings for the hall were taken by the chemist, Mr Balmer, from his shop on Upper Main Street.

The Parish Church bells have summoned the faithful to worship for over a century. Said to be amongst the hundred heaviest in the world, the largest is 1.25 metres (49.5 inches) in diameter and weighs over a ton. Only during the Second World War were the bells kept deliberately silent, although they were rung out in joy at the end of both World Wars. In sorrow, muffled peals have also been rung on the death of prominent Bangorians as well as royalty and politicians. Across the road from the Parish Church is Wesley Centenary Methodist Church, built in 1891. The building to its left in the postcard view was originally the manse, now the site of the minor hall. Dr James Robertson was the minister at Wesley Centenary from 1903 to 1906. Charles Milligan recalled an occasion when a member of the congregation had been looking at his pocket watch. During a moment of complete silence the gentleman closed his watch case and the sound echoed all round the church. Dr Robertson stopped, looked down the church and said, "If you want to know the time it's 7.15. I will be finished at 7.30, will that do you?".

Carnegie Library and Technical School, Hamilton Road

Posted 22 August 1913
*Publisher: Eason & Son Ltd,
Dublin & Belfast*

Carnegie Library & Technical School, Bangor.

The earliest reference to a library in Bangor comes from the Ordnance Survey Memoirs of 1837, in which it was reported that "There is one library in the town, consisting of a limited number of religious and moral works". By the turn of the twentieth century, the new Urban District Council felt that Bangor needed "a free library to bring them up on even lines with other seaside resorts". Scottish born steel magnate and philanthropist, Andrew Carnegie, gave £1,250 towards the construction of the new library and the Hon Somerset Ward provided the land on which it was to be built. When opened by the Marquess of Londonderry on 8 January 1910, the library and reading room were located on the ground floor, with the Municipal Technical School above. Posted just three years after the building was completed, the sender wrote to Miss M Morton at Riversdale House, Doagh, "Having a good time here. It is very hot. Expect to see you on Monday. Yours &c., HB".

In all, 2,509 Carnegie libraries were built between 1883 and 1929, including 660 in Britain and Ireland. The 1938 *Official Guide to Bangor* says of the library that its location, within the grounds of Ward Park, gives it the "advantage of the most pleasing surroundings that a building devised to be central could have in Bangor". The guide also advises that visitors to Bangor could avail themselves of the "privilege of using the Lending Department on their giving reasonable security". The Technical School expanded into nearby Hamilton House in 1949, moving to new premises on Castle Park Road in 1967. In 2007 the Carnegie Library was closed while a major refurbishment and extension got underway, with temporary library facilities provided in the Flagship Centre. Reopened in November 2008, the Arts and Crafts building of 1910 now houses the children's library on the ground floor and the reference library above, while the vast extension to the south now includes facilities such as self service kiosks, an exhibition space and an IT suite equipped with 44 computers.

Ward Park looking towards the lower pond

12. Ward Park from Main Entrance, Bangor, Co. Down.

Posted 27 July 1915
Publisher: Hurst & Co, Belfast

Before Ward Park was created in 1909 it had been the site of a brickworks. This view was taken from the main entrance at Hamilton Road, originally provided with iron gates which would be shut each night, but which were removed during the Second World War. In the days when the park was still a brickfield, a magnesium well known as 'My Lady's Well' was situated about 40 yards from the present Hamilton Road entrance. Water from this spring well was considered a perfect accompaniment to whiskey, and connoisseurs of the best single malts at the nearby Castle Arms took it in turns to draw water from it. The sender of this card, addressed to Mrs William S Speer of Harmoney Hall, Ballycraigy, Carnmoney, wrote that she was "Having a jolly old time down here. Lovely weather these last two days. Great crowds of people".

A Castle Arms patron composed a skit about My Lady's Well and its spa water, which was "full of something which covered the inside of a glass with a mass of small crystals". The whiskey lover, who was also on the staff of the *Belfast Telegraph*, wrote that the brickfield spa water was "delicious" with whiskey and was also "unequalled for cooking the national murphies, or for mixing punch and it will wash clothes of itself. Professor Blimey an eminent authority says it is a charming hectic, dietetic, diabetic, diuretic, tartar emetic water of the first class". The well was covered over when Ward Park was created, and the Castle Arms 'Jolly Topers' drinking club had to look elsewhere for their water.

Ward Park looking towards Prospect Road

Ward Park. Bangor Co Down

Posted 7 September 1927
Publisher: Unknown

In this excellent view we see the gun of the German submarine UB-19. The gun was presented by the Admiralty to Bangor in 1919, honouring Barry Bingham, a son of Lord and Lady Clanmorris of Bangor Castle, who won the Victoria Cross for his brave actions at the Battle of Jutland. In the distance at centre is Hamilton Road Presbyterian Church, opened in 1899. The vestibule and tower were not added until 1966, so this view shows the utilitarian brick frontage, a 'temporary' feature which endured for almost seven decades. The houses at far left are on Springfield Avenue, which was developed a few years before the park was laid out. 'Nellie' writes to Miss M Douse of Chestnut Lodge, Booterstown, Co Dublin, that "There are some lovely spots around here. I do not feel like coming home at all".

Photographer:
Nigel Snell

The U-boat gun was made by Friedrich Krupp AG in 1916, the same year Barry Bingham distinguished himself at Jutland. Bingham's VC, one of relatively few awarded for naval bravery, is consequently very rare. It was purchased by North Down Borough Council at Sotheby's in 1983, and is now in North Down Museum. The postcard opposite was sent the year the War Memorial was unveiled on a site directly behind the photographer. Featuring a bronze figure of Erin laying a palm frond at the foot of a stone obelisk, the Memorial was also to have included Nike, the Winged Goddess of Victory, but she was never added. Beside the lower pond at right, "beloved of small boys with yachts", is Bangor Carnegie Library, built to the designs of Ernest L Woods in 1910, but now greatly extended.

Ward Park from the upper ponds

THE CENTRAL GARDENS, BANGOR

Posted 9 August 1912
Publisher: EA Schwerdtfeger & Co, London

Although laid out in 1909, the new public park was not christened 'Ward Park' until 1912. The stream was expanded to form three lakes, crossed by a number of rustic bridges, one of which is seen here in the foreground. As well as the introduction of waterfowl, "the feeding of which is a constant pleasure both to young and old", the park was also in time provided with an aviary, a bandstand, bowling greens, a putting green, tennis courts and a children's play area. At left can be seen the glazed roof lantern of Hamilton Road Presbyterian Church,

and at right is the original clubhouse of Bangor Golf Club, opened in 1904 a year after the club was founded. Sent to Miss Martin of Dundee, the message reads, "Dear Daisy. You are having a fine holiday. No matter whom I speak to, everyone seems to have had a card from you. Dear Daisy will you ever settle again. I am suffering at present from a bad cold, but hope to be alright in a few days. Just in my head. Flying about too much has been the cause. Love to all".

Photographer:
Adam Bell

The *Official Guide to Bangor* of 1935 commented that "The park is very tastefully laid out, an ornament to the whole district, a pleasure-ground for young and old, an example, in many parts of it, of how a garden should be kept, and a healthy open-air space secured for the townspeople for all time, in the centre of the town". And so it remains today! When nearby Williamson's Farm came up for sale in 1933, the lands were bought by Bangor Golf Club, who commissioned designs for a new course and, in 1935, moved out of the original Edwardian clubhouse into a new Modernist one off Broadway. Moira Drive was built where the 1st fairway had once been, and during the Second World War the old course was also used to grow vegetables. The former clubhouse became Aubrey House School from the mid 1930s. During the war it housed the local ATS unit, and afterwards was home to Connor House Preparatory School, before being demolished in 1970.

Lower Main Street looking from the crest of the hill

Main Street, Bangor (Co Down).   RELIABLE SERIES No. 8078

Unposted, about 1905–1907
Publisher: William Ritchie & Sons Ltd

The first two buildings on the left, nos 70–72, were the site of Smyth & McClure's grocery shop. Next is 'Scrabo House' with its distinctive chamfered corner and Dutch gable. The proprietor, James Conolly, sold stationery, fancy goods and souvenirs as well as running a lending library. James Conolly published his own series of postcards, some of which feature in this book. Just round the corner on King Street (known as West Street until about 1910) was Hugh Furey's bar and off-licence. Furey also ran a 'high class grocers' at 62–64 Main Street, the back yard of which was shared with the pub. Tom Hoey started work at Furey's age 15 in 1957. He remembers, "Lots of well-to-do people shopped there. You had to go round and pick off the shelves everything the customer wanted, write it on a bill, add it up, and send it and the money on a catapult system to the cash office. We packed our own label tea and cut cheeses and bacon to the customers' requirements".

The group of tall gable-fronted buildings at centre right, built in 1889 for James Neill, are the most prominent survivors in this modern view. Just up from here, the buildings at nos 49–63 were all rebuilt following two car bomb attacks in 1972. WA Gilbey wine & spirit merchant occupied nos 53–55, now the Sally hair and beauty shop. A bill in the author's collection, issued by WA Gilbey in 1910, politely asks that the recipient "be so kind as to let me know by return if Mr Climenson can possibly pay above account. A reply would so much oblige". Butcher David Allen, just a few doors down at no 47, was also owed money by Spencer Climenson. His patience evidently wearing thin, David Allen wrote on his bill, "Dear Sir. You did not send on cheque as you promised on Tuesday. I think it is too bad when all the other creditors got a share. I think I was entitled to mine. Be kind enough to send it on in full at once & oblige".

Lower Main Street looking towards Woolworth's

MAIN STREET, BANGOR.

Unposted, about early 1950s
*Publisher: Gordon & Co,
14 Waterloo Park, Belfast*

A busy scene has been captured in this colourful summer view, dating to about the early 1950s. In the foreground we see a woman walking with her bicycle, fitted with a wicker basket for carrying bits of shopping. "During the summer season," recalls Gary Graham, "Main Street could be so packed with holiday people that sometimes it was quicker to walk on the road". The Central Café, opposite Trinity Church, was owned by Angelo Togneri and was popular with American soldiers billeted in the Trinity Church halls during the Second World War. Angelo kept chickens at the back of the Café, towards the Vennel, and Winnie Graham, who worked there in the 1940s, was often allowed to take an egg home, at a time when eggs were scarce. The gabled building displaying a pair of large Union Flags was Woolworth's, which opened in Bangor in 1930 as a '3d and 6d store'. Just down from Woolworth's was Lennon's fruit shop, fondly remembered by many.

Photographer:
Henry Doggart

Apart from a few buildings towards the bottom of the street, little remains today of the built environment depicted opposite, the exception being Oxfam, trading from the surviving half of a building dated to about 1890. The former Wellworth's supermarket was built a few doors up from Woolworth's in the mid 1960s. Woolworth's, having been rebuilt and enlarged in 1958, occupied the same site until December 2008 when the firm went into administration and all 807 of its UK stores were closed. Just out of view, to the right of Trinity Presbyterian Church is a squat building put up in the mid 1960s. In 1912 this was the site of Bangor's first cinema, the Picture House, which reopened in 1928 as the Adelphi. With a capacity of over 600, the Adelphi advertised as the "centre of first-class talkies" in the 1930s, its "modern sound equipment" ensuring "faithful reproduction of vocal and instrumental sound for patrons".

Lower Main Street looking towards the Sunken Gardens

Main Street, Bangor.

Posted 14 October 1949
Publisher: Unknown

On the corner of Main Street and Queen's Parade is John Lynch's Central Bar. Built about 1895, it replaced a whitewashed single storey building which may have been one of the "80 newe houses" built by Sir James Hamilton in the early years of the seventeenth century. The two storey building opposite Lynch's bar was built about 1890 as the Eagle Hotel, later becoming the Yachtsman Hotel. To its right was Lightbody's, a family owned grocery shop and restaurant which was replaced by a Co-op superstore in 1965. Beyond Main Street is the Sunken Gardens, with the North Pier visible in the distance. Sent to Miss Betty Hogg of Bridge Street, Larne, Dorothy and Sammy write, "Having a wonderful time. Weather not so good. See you soon".

Much of Lower Main Street has been rebuilt in the last six decades. Thankfully the former Lynch's Bar, now a popular café and restaurant, has managed to survive despite the dual threat posed by Troubles era terrorists on the one hand and developers on the other. Another rare survivor from the 1890s is the Wesley Hall, just out of view to the left of the photographer. On the right is the Flagship Centre, built on the site of the former gasworks and 1960s Co-op. Opened in November 1993, phase one of the £20 million Flagship included anchor tenants Dunnes Stores and a brand new Co-op superstore which promised to "bring new standards of food shopping to the town", including special bakery, delicatessen and fish counters, "the widest range of frozen foods in N. Ireland" and state of the art conveniences like "full itemised receipts from laser-scanning tills". Adams childrenswear, Connors chemist, Stewart Millar newsagents, Treasure Cove gifts, Bijou jewellery and the Post Office were among the other early tenants. The Flagship later extended its Main Street frontage to absorb the adjoining two storey buildings, nos 1–5, visible in the postcard view.

The Esplanade

THE PARADE, BANGOR, CO. DOWN.

Posted about 1907–1909
Publisher: Frederick Hartmann

The area to the left of this image was once occupied by a row of buildings known as the Parade, including a 50 foot high cotton mill built in 1806. In the early 1890s Bangor's Town Commissioners acquired the land and demolished the old buildings, creating in its place the Esplanade, an area enclosed by iron railings, provided with a bandstand and ornamental drinking fountain. This was a popular place for summer entertainments such as concert parties and troupes of Pierrots. In this pleasant postcard view, transport is entirely of the horse driven kind. In the foreground a driver has stopped at a water trough so that his horse may slake its thirst. Sent to CB Hart Esq of Lisnacree, Strandtown, Belfast about 1907–1909 (the stamp was carefully removed for the recipient's stamp collection) AJ Kirk wrote, "Irene and I are having a grand time. We are going round to the Hobby Horses now for a ride. I had a lovely tea etc & think Mrs C's is just lovely". The hobby horses were a popular attraction at Clifton from the 1890s. In 1915 the Urban District Council acquired the land there and laid out Kingsland.

The Esplanade became the Sunken Gardens in the 1930s, and it was again remodelled more recently when the Marina development was undertaken. The only remaining feature from the 1890s is the cast iron drinking fountain, erected by the members of Bangor Corinthian Sailing Club (est 1881) in memory of Mrs Arthur Hill Coates. The bandstand, the cost of which had been defrayed by the Hon RE Ward of Bangor Castle, was moved to Marine Gardens in 1915. In its place rose the Ballycullen stone McKee clock, paid for by a gift of £200 from James McKee, the Borough Rates Collector. In place of the horse trough, an important part of Edwardian transport provision, are today's transport necessities, traffic lights and a pedestrian crossing! The buildings occupying the southern end of Quay Street remain the same as in 1905, although their uses have changed. Built in 1866, the building now occupied by the Petty Sessions Court was originally the Belfast Bank, while its three storey red brick neighbour the Palladium was built about 1895 as E & W Pim's grocery emporium.

McKee clock and putting green

McKee Clock and Putting Green, Bangor, Co. Down, N.I.   Colour Photo by John Hinde, F.R.P.S.

Posted 26 July 1971
*Publisher: John Hinde Ltd,
Cabinteely, Co Dublin
Photographer: John Hinde*

The Esplanade was remodelled in the late 1930s as the 'Sunken Gardens', featuring colourful displays of annual bedding plants. A red brick shelter and ice cream kiosk were also added at this time, as was the putting green beside the McKee clock. In this view Pickie Pool can be seen across the bay and behind the McKee clock on the South Pier is an outdoor amusement park operated by Barry's. In the distance at far right a large electric crane stands at the end of the Central Pier.

It replaced an earlier steam driven crane in the early 1950s. Sent by a visitor from the west of the province, the author of this postcard tells Miss H McCullagh of Drumcose, Enniskillen, "Arrived safely yesterday. Weather is only mixed middling. I see a good many Fermanagh cars but no one that I know so far". The Fermanagh visitor was staying at Mrs M Hawthorne's guest house at 74 Seacliff Road.

Cherie Bell recalls happy childhood days in the 1960s, getting candyfloss from the kiosk, "I remember watching mesmerised as the girl poured in **bags** of sugar and then put a stick into the spinning drum to collect the wisps of 'floss'. It usually ended up stuck to your mouth and all round your face!" The 'Kiddie Land' amusements on the South Pier, including Minnie Delino's 'Peter Pan Railway', miniature carousels and swingboats, were a popular attraction for almost 30 years, until the pier reverted to its original commercial use in 1982. The area was completely redeveloped around 1990 as part of the marina scheme, although the McKee clock and the ornamental drinking fountain canopy remain. About where the ice cream kiosk once was is now a taxi rank, but ice cream is still a much anticipated treat for summer visitors, as seen here in the form of a 'Mrs Whippy' van, the side of which advertises that "Karina's ices are the best".

Ballymagee Street looking east

Ballymagee Street, Bangor.

Posted 7 July 1907
Publisher: G Lowden & Co, Bangor

Shown on the Raven map of 1625, Ballymagee Street, renamed High Street about 1926, is one of the oldest streets in Bangor. The curved buildings at its foot date to about 1860. At right, on the corner with Bridge Street, is the Criterion public house, which advertises "Stabling", "Cycle Sheds" and "Belfast Prices". The next building up on the right was the Alexandra Hotel, but it later became Thompson's outfitters. Natalie Murphy recalls that "The ladies in Thompson's were very determined salespeople. If you dared to make for the door without spending, you generally got a comment like 'All those lovely clothes and she couldn't find anything!'" Past McKeown's Central Fish Hall with its carved wooden fish hanging above the shopfront is a low two storey building of about 1850, probably now the oldest surviving building on the street. This postcard was sent to Lieutenant Sarah Black of the Salvation Army in Worcester, South Africa. The message reads, "I have been waiting this long time for a letter from you. Does this P. Card remind you of good old times? Love from Meg S.C. Gray's Hill".

Photographer:
Adam Bell

Happily the distinctive rounded corner buildings are still a feature of the lower part of the street. On the left hand side, Café Ceol now occupies the site which was home to the Ulster Arms pub for about a century. Further up the street, staying on the left, are two more pubs worthy of mention. The Ormeau Arms, commonly known as Fealty's, is a fine example of a Victorian corner pub complete with central door. Next but one to Fealty's is Bangor's oldest public house, Jenny Watts. Known for many years as the 'Old House at Home', the history of this pub is reputed to stretch back as far as 1780. Charles Milligan recalled a 'jarvey' (a colloquial name for the driver of a jaunting car) who was known to frequent the Old House at Home on Saturday nights. "At closing time", remembered Charles, "they would bring him out, put him across the car, give the horse a pat on the back and it would bring him home". The jarvey lived on a lane behind Dufferin Villas at the east end of Ballyholme Bay.

Ballymagee Street looking west

Ballymagee Street, Bangor.

Erin! Oh Erin! Though long in the shade,
Thy star shall shine out when the proudest shall fade.

Posted about 1910
*Publisher: Eason & Son Ltd,
Dublin & Belfast*

One of the Reliance Motor Service's new charabancs is seen trundling down the hill on its return journey from Donaghadee. The company began in 1908 and offered trips to Donaghadee and back for a shilling. Unable to manage the steep gradient of High Street, these early charabancs set off from outside the Royal Hotel on Quay Street, making their way along Seacliff Road. There was of course no problem coming down High Street, on the return journey! Where the pedestrians are at left is the corner of Alfred Street; an enamel sign displayed there advertises 'Singer Sewing Machines'. Addressed to Miss McBurney of Dundee, the message reads, "How are you dear Jenny? I have been for writing you every day but always something turned up to put me off, I am ashamed to say. Well now I am here yet after having a glorious time spring cleaning. Oh what a time. You will be busy removing it is a job. I will write you soon Jenny, letting you know everything. Lots to say. Always your A.S.M.".

Whereas the lower end of High Street has been predominantly commercial since at least the 1890s, the upper part remained largely residential until the mid twentieth century. In 1970 there were still around a dozen dwelling houses on High Street, but two decades later only one remained. Just out of shot at far right, no 89 was the last remaining house; it became the Toucan off-licence about 1990. However, unlike Main Street, which has suffered at the hands of terrorist bombs and schemes aimed at 'modernisation' and 'improvement', High Street still retains many of its old buildings and, as a consequence, a great deal more character. Visible at the bottom of the street in the view opposite is the bandstand, which was replaced by the McKee clock in 1915.

The Grand Hotel, Quay Street

Unposted, about 1905
Publisher: Unknown, probably Mrs Annie O'Hara
Printer: The Advertisement PC Co, London

With its crowstepped gables, conical corner turrets and ornate cast iron balconies, the Grand Hotel was Bangor's select establishment, occupying a "beautiful and bracing position" overlooking the newly created Esplanade pleasure grounds. It was built for Mrs Annie O'Hara about 1895, replacing a row of sea captain's houses. Muriel Breen recalled going to a children's charity fancy dress ball at the Grand in the early years of the twentieth century, "I'll never forget walking into the magical place with its balloons, fairy lights and musical band in the distance". Muriel was dressed as a chrysanthemum, but the judges "didn't seem impressed", a boy dressed as a letter box and a girl dressed

as a mermaid picking up first prizes. The Grand was purchased in 1910 by a syndicate "interested in the cause of temperance" and it became a teetotal establishment. For some years it was even run as a home for underprivileged boys, until in the 1930s Ernest and Louisa Barry transformed the former hotel into Barry's Amusements. About 1945 Minnie Delino, daughter of Ernest and Louisa, took over. Many Bangor folk remember Mrs Delino as a colourful character who always carried a large bunch of keys, with which she was known to give naughty boys a good whack round the head!

The building to the left of the Grand Hotel started its life as the Burlington Restaurant, but it is best remembered as the 700 seat Picture Palace, where patrons enjoyed cinematographic thrills in sumptuous surroundings, the grand staircase in the entrance hall leading to "a fine balcony" with "red plush seats". William Wilson recalled his childhood in the 1920s, a "chief delight" of which was to go to the Picture Palace matinee on Saturdays; "When the lights went out there was a huge cheer … I will never forget seeing Charlie Chaplin eating his boot in *The Gold Rush*". Frances Murphy recalls the excitement one Christmas when word got about that children attending the Palace would be given a tangerine wrapped in silver paper. Gutted by fire in 1940, the Palace never reopened as a cinema, although the Windsor bar which occupied part of the building remains to this day. Meanwhile Barry's, famous for its dodgems and coin operated amusements, including 'What the Butler Saw' and animated tableaux showing haunted houses and gruesome executions, brought joy to generations of children until the building and its contents were sold in 1982. Demolished in 1984, the site lay vacant for a decade until the Marine Court Hotel was built.

The Royal Hotel, Quay Street

Royal Hotel, Bangor. 381

Posted 3 October 1949
Publisher: Millar and Lang

About eight feet up on the Crosby Street gable of the Royal Hotel is an inscription, carved in stone, which reads "Built by Iame [James] Lyons in the year of Our Lord 1773". This refers to the three storey predecessor of the present building, which can be seen at far left on page 62. When Harry McFall became the owner in the mid nineteenth century, he decided to call his new hotel the Royal. In addition to being a hotelier, the energetic McFall was also Harbourmaster, Poor Law Guardian, Secretary to Bangor Gas Company, agent for Hope Mutual Life and owner of livery stables. Addressed to Miss J Russell at Banbridge, the sender of this postcard wrote "17 Southwell Road. Everything is going on satisfactorily and I am very happy. I do all the cooking etc. Love L.B.". What at first seems an odd message for a holidaymaker might be explained if the sender was employed by Mrs Hunter, proprietor of the guesthouse at 17 Southwell Road, to help with the cooking and other domestic chores?

The Royal Hotel was bought in 1908 by William O'Hara, son of Mrs Annie O'Hara who owned the Grand Hotel nearby. In 1932, having acquired the two storey building to the south, the Royal was rebuilt and extended. The new hotel, advertised as "Unsurpassed for comfort and food" boasted 50 bedrooms with hot and cold water, lifts to all floors, spacious dining rooms and no less than eight billiard tables. During the Second World War Bangor was designated a convoy assembly and dispersal point, and the Royal Hotel's upper floors were taken over by naval personnel. Ownership remained with the O'Hara family until the mid 1990s, when local businessman and owner of the neighbouring Windsor bar, Paul Donegan, bought the Royal. Today Paul Donegan has ambitious plans to develop a brand new hotel and apartments on the site but, for the time being, the elegant building with a hint of Art Deco remains a familiar sight on Bangor's seafront.

The Old Pier

The Old Pier, Bangor, Co. Down

26364

Posted 22 July 1907
Publisher: Valentine, Dublin

The brigantine seen berthed at the 'Old Pier' is the collier *Bellewood*, owned until 1904 by Mrs Olivia Neill, widow of the coal merchant Charles Neill. Coal from Cumberland, Ayrshire or the Mersey was among the chief imports to Bangor, along with limestone from Whitehead or Glenarm, and bricks. This pier was also used by the paddle steamers *Erin* and *Bangor Castle,* operated by the Moore Brothers from 1864 and 1873 respectively, hence the wall down the middle, to separate passengers from the messiness of cargo imports.

Moore Bros were proud of their safety record, carrying thousands of passengers from and to Belfast each year "without the slightest mishap", a record attributed in 1885 to the fact that "The captains and officers of both steamers are teetotallers". Sent to Master Martin Poots at the Post Office, Newcastle, Co Down, 'Vita' wrote, "Please tell S. to come to Bangor when she comes home. Is Daisy's toe better? Give my love to Aunt and Florrie".

Photographer:
Deborah and May Carvill

Moore Bros' monopoly came to an end when the Belfast and Co Down Railway started a competing service in the 1890s. The *Slieve Bearnagh* was the BCDR's new paddle steamer, operating the Belfast to Bangor route from 1896 until 1911. In 1895 a new pier had been constructed to the north and the pier shown in the postcard became the 'Old Pier', also known as the Central Pier. It reverted to the discharge of cargoes and the dividing wall was eventually removed. The *Bellewood* was in fact Bangor's last sailing collier, replaced by faster steam powered vessels. Olivia Neill's son and grandson, both called Charles, continued in the coal trade until their business was taken over by Cawoods. Today an area of reclaimed land comprising a car park, boat repair yard and the Bregenz House complex, home to the Maritime and Coastguard Agency, occupies the former location of the Central Pier, which was rebuilt further out into the bay. The last coal boat sailed into Bangor in 1987 and in 1990 the *Greeba River* was the last general cargo coaster to load from the Central Pier extension, however, fishing boats are still a common sight in the harbour.

The New Pier

New Pier, Bangor Co. Down

Unposted, about 1905
Publisher: W Lawrence, Dublin

In 1890–1891 the paddle steamers which plied the busy route between Belfast's Donegall Quay and Bangor were responsible for landing 600,000 passengers at Bangor. As the existing pier was not suited to this volume of traffic, the Town Commissioners approached RE Ward to commence discussions over the construction of a new pier, reserved for the conveyance of passengers only. Costing £24,000, the first 420 feet of the New Pier was concrete and the remaining 500 feet open form, the pitch pine for which was specially imported from Pensacola, Florida. By 1895 the fine New Pier was complete and at its end it was even furnished with a bandstand. In this view we see the concrete section; the timber structure continued round to the right. H & J Martin were the contractors for the New Pier or the 'North Pier' as it became known. Their name and the date, 1895, are embossed on bollards still in situ to this day.

Photographer:
Deborah Carvill

April 1914 saw 80 tons of German bought rifles landed at the North Pier, part of a scheme masterminded by the Ulster Volunteer Force amid a deepening Home Rule crisis. Cloak and dagger operations conducted by starlight were, however, the exception to the rule, and the North Pier continued its more usual role as a berth for passenger steamers until 1939. A violent storm in 1947 caused considerable damage to the open form section, and in the decades which followed it became ever more rickety, so much so that the council put up railings to discourage people from venturing onto it. In 1980 the wooden section was removed altogether and work commenced on the construction of a new breakwater, the first phase of the marina development which would see Bangor Bay transformed within a decade. When the old support timbers were drawn out of the seabed, it was discovered that they had only been driven in about six feet! The North Breakwater was complete by the mid 1980s and in 2005 it was officially renamed the Eisenhower Pier, honouring Dwight D Eisenhower who, as Supreme Allied Commander in Europe, visited Bangor in the lead up to the Normandy Landings of 1944.

Rowing boats alongside the Harbourmaster's Office

BANGOR FROM PIER.

Posted 13 September 1917
Publisher: A Mencarelli, Boulevard, Bangor

Published by A Mencarelli of the Boulevard café, Bridge Street, this postcard shows rowing boats for hire at the east of Bangor Bay, viewed from the New Pier of 1895. A total of 120 licences were issued for rowing boats within the harbour limits, the greatest number being held by Lenaghen and his successor Laird on the opposite side of the bay. However, on this side, William Caulfield was licensed to operate 25 boats, as were Harvey & Brown. At night, some of the boats would be hauled up the slip to the basement of the Harbourmaster's Office and the remainder anchored in the bay, tied up in pairs. If the weather was bad, they were rowed into the Long Hole, passing under the bridge at the entrance to the North Pier, which was blocked off in about the mid 1950s. Tom Hoey, who worked for Billy Caulfield as a teenager, recalls having to row along the coast, accompanied by one or two mates, searching for boats abandoned by daytrippers, who would sometimes go ashore at Crawfordsburn or Helen's Bay and get the train home! After rowing the boats back to Bangor, Tom and his mates would treat themselves to a plate of hot peas at Tony's café at the bottom of High Street.

Photographer:
Deborah Carvill

Today the rowing boats of Caulfield and Laird are long gone, the nearest modern equivalent being the swan pedaloes at Pickie Fun Park. Visitors would, however, have a challenge propelling one of the swans up the coast, as they are contained within their own boating lake! Where seawater once lapped, at the edge of the Harbourmaster's Office, is now a sea of tarmacadam home to a fleet of cars, and the office itself is now a restaurant. Behind can be seen the distinctive crowstep gable and battlemented corner tower of Bangor's oldest surviving building, the Custom House erected in 1637. In the nineteenth century the building was the residence of Harbourmaster David Harvey, and by the 1880s it functioned as the summer studio of the "celebrated photographic artist" Robert Seggons of Belfast. Hot salt and fresh water baths were installed in 1933, "guaranteed to relieve rheumatism, sciatica and other disorders" but the baths welcomed their last customers in 1954 and the building was thereafter an antique shop. Today known as Tower House, it has been home to a Tourist Information Centre since 1983.

Queen's Parade

THE PARADE, BANGOR, CO. DOWN.

Posted 2 March 1952
Publisher: Valentine & Sons Ltd

Photographed on the eve of the Second World War, this wonderful postcard view shows Quay Street, Bridge Street, Main Street, Queen's Parade and Gray's Hill, with the South Pier and Sunken Gardens in the foreground. A 'stop me and buy one' ice cream vendor stands by the lamppost at bottom left, waiting for his next customer. Caproni's and Luchi's were well known for their ice cream, but this vendor is selling 'Frozen Joy' made by Montgomery & Nesbitt of Bingham Street Lane. The low rectangular building beside the putting green in the foreground housed public toilets as well as a kiosk for the green, an information bureau and a booking office for motor coach tours. The sender of this card urged Mrs C Abery of Reading, Berkshire, to "Listen in to the Light Programme on Monday evening at 8 o'clock – if you're in".

Photographer:
Deborah and May Carvill

In this colourful modern view the funfair has taken up residence for the summer where the putting green once was. Unlike the earlier view, awnings are now a rare sight on Main Street, David Mawhinney's butchers at no 78 being about the last to sport one. Whereas the sea was previously a stone's throw from Queen's Parade, the marina development has pushed it back about 60 metres. On the flipside, the breakwaters constructed as part of the marina scheme in the 1980s ensure the seafront is no longer at the mercy of winter gales. Prior to this, stormy seas proved an irresistible temptation for generations of thrill seeking boys who would run along the sea wall, ducking the waves as they smashed overhead. In 1999 Marcus Patton noted that "Lack of investment during the development of the marina has been followed by compulsory acquisition of properties on the main Parade, which are currently demolished or boarded up awaiting comprehensive redevelopment". Over a decade on, little progress has been made.

Queen's Parade looking east

BG 13   QUEENS PARADE, BANGOR, CO. DOWN, N. IRELAND   A TUCK CARD

Posted 7 August 1957
Publisher: Raphael Tuck & Sons Ltd

Hordes of visitors throng Queen's Parade in this view from the 1950s. The sea wall, its sandstone coping weathered by the crashing waves of angry winter seas, was in the summer months a popular place to meet up with friends or just sit and watch the world go by. "At the weekends especially, groups of girls would promenade along the Parade past groups of boys", recalls Tom Hoey, "all in good fun". The location suggests the photographer may have captured this busy scene from an upper floor window at Caproni's café, one of three Caproni establishments in the town, the others being the Locarno café further along Queen's Parade where 'fish teas' (fish and chips, tea, bread and butter) could be enjoyed for 2/- 3d, and the legendary ballroom and Mirimar Café at Ballyholme. Mr and Mrs Chapman sent this postcard to Mr and Mrs Riddell of Corbridge, Northumberland, writing, "I have forsaken England this year for Ireland. I think we have been wise because so far we have missed the thunder storms & are having glorious weather".

Photographer:
Deborah Carvill

This view was taken from the offices of North Down YMCA, formerly Caproni's café, where patrons once enjoyed sea views. Today the view is of a car park, albeit set within surprisingly verdant surroundings. Worth noting in the postcard view are the miniature lights strung between the lampposts. From June until the end of October the seafront was once illuminated by "myriads of coloured electric lamps" giving the bay a "festive and fairylike appearance". 7 May 1930 was the day electricity came to Bangor and a huge crowd packed the seafront, eager to see the "coloured light festoons" switched on at 10pm. Dignitaries including the Prime Minister of Northern Ireland, Lord Craigavon, assembled for a dinner before the event. 10pm came and went and the assembled crowds started to become restless, the night being an exceptionally cold one with a biting north westerly wind. Meanwhile the great and the good continued to give after dinner speeches in the comfort of their hotel, finally emerging at 11.15pm. When Lord Craigavon ascended the platform at the end of Queen's Parade and came forward to speak, a voice from the crowd shouted out "Switch the b***** lights on and let us go home" and he did just that!

Bangor Bay and Queen's Parade

QUEEN'S PARADE, BANGOR C° DOWN.

Unposted, 1920
Publisher: Hurst & Co, Belfast

The beach in the foreground was popularly known as the 'Steps' beach because of the steps which led down to it from opposite Southwell Road. The sand here was considered to be particularly suited for sandcastles and competitions were regularly held for the best sand designs. In the 1920s and 1930s, first prize was often a *Chums* children's annual and runners up might get a sandcastle bucket filled with toffees. Further along, the beach in the far corner was called the 'Slip' beach after the slipway which led down to it from street level. It was here that the stream which flows through Ward Park drained into the sea, and adventurous children would sometimes explore as far as a couple of hundred yards along the tunnel. Even the sea wall itself provided opportunities for fun; Gary Graham recalls, "For a dare we as boys had to jump off the wall down onto the sand, perhaps 15 feet below". Although unposted, the original owner of this postcard wrote on the back, "Bought at Bangor, 11.8.20".

Photographer:
Deborah Carvill

Queen's Parade runs along the original shore of Bangor Bay from the bottom of Main Street towards Pickie. The stretch of the Parade from Gray's Hill along to Pickie was commonly known as the Kinnegar, the name being derived from a coney or rabbit warren shown to have occupied that area on the Raven maps of 1625. Formerly called Sandy Row, Queen's Parade was renamed when King Edward VII and Queen Alexandra visited Bangor in July 1903. It was also at this time that Fisher Hill became Victoria Road. To celebrate the coronation of Edward VII in August 1902, Bangor Urban District Council obtained an "old time wooden schooner" which was to be set alight at sea. The ageing ship, laden with wood shavings, barrels of tar, a barrel of paraffin oil and other combustibles "went up like a bomb", much to the delight of the crowds which had travelled far and wide to witness the spectacle. Today a burning boat would be a cause for alarm in Bangor Marina, but the bay is still a favourite setting for celebrations, fireworks being the accepted modern equivalent.

Pickie

THE PICKIE, BANGOR.

Posted 15 July 1925
Publisher: WA Green, Belfast

In this busy view several hundred people can be seen enjoying a stroll at Pickie. At far right is the entrance to Marine Gardens, acquired by the Urban District Council as part of the Bangor Water and Improvement Act of 1905. In 1885 WG Lyttle wrote that Bangor exhibited "all the evidences of increasing prosperity" in the form of "constant and ever-increasing additions to the chastely designed, elegant villas overspreading the landscape, and occupying hill and vale and points of vantage on every side". The terrace seen here at left is Mount Pleasant and to its right is Martello, undoubtedly one of the "chastely designed, elegant villas" so admired by Lyttle. The grand villa to the right of Martello is Augustaville, built by Robert Russell about 1887. 'Lenaghen's Boats' is painted on the seaward side of the wall in the middle distance. The rocky foreshore here, complete with its own small jetty, was where James Lenaghen of 'Brookfield', Southwell Road, hired out rowing boats. Jimmy Laird took over from Lenaghen in the 1940s.

Photographer:
Gerry Coe

Jimmy Laird was licensed to hire 60 rowing boats from the Pickie side of Bangor Bay. He also offered short pleasure cruises aboard his motor boats, which he built himself. Laird was 82 when he built his last passenger motor boat. In total he built 12 for himself, all of which were named after his wife Alice, as well as 25 for other customers. When not in use, Laird's rowing boats were stacked upside down on wooden frames, which Frances Murphy recalls were ideal for attempting childhood gymnastic feats, including turning head over heels. For Gary Graham, Laird's jetty brings back a childhood memory he will never forget. It was World War Two and young Gary spotted an aeroplane flying overhead. While staring skyward in an attempt to determine if it was "one of ours" he fell off Laird's jetty, where he happened to be standing. Soaked head to foot, the unlucky boy "squelched all the way home" to Central Street. The jetty was removed in 1987 during construction of the marina.

Bryansburn Road and Gray's Hill

Bryansburn Road, Bangor, Co. Down

Grey's Hill, Bangor, Co. Down.

Until the late nineteenth century, Crawfordsburn Road also included present day Bryansburn Road and Central Avenue, providing a direct link between Bangor's Main Street and Crawfordsburn, with nothing but fields in between. When villas began to be built there from the 1890s, 'Bryansburn Road' was born, taking its name from the stream at its western end, which flows under it and down through Strickland's Glen to the sea. Although Gray's Hill can be seen on the first Ordnance Survey map of Bangor in 1833, it had not yet acquired its name. In *Reminiscences of Old Bangor*, Charlie Seyers wrote that "A man called Gray was supposed to be the first to build in Gray's Hill and the street was named after him". Indeed, a slate headstone in Bangor Abbey graveyard is inscribed as having been "Erected by James Gray of Gray's Hill, in memory of his wife Sarah Gray, who died 10th Feby. 1834 aged 56 years". Also remembered are "two children who died young", sons Charles and John, daughter Margaret and James himself, who died 6 March 1859 aged 77.

Unposted, about 1910
Publisher: James Conolly, Scrabo House, Bangor

Characterised by substantial, solidly built houses of the late Victorian and Edwardian eras, Bryansburn Road has suffered in recent years from what the Ulster Architectural Heritage Society dubbed in 2000 "developer-itis", although the 'Credit Crunch' would seem to have considerably stemmed the flow. Gray's Hill was, until the mid 1930s, home to the Bangor branch of the Belfast Co-operative Society Ltd, where shoppers could purchase "groceries, provisions and drapery goods". When it moved into the new Bank of Ireland building on Main Street in 1937, it also boasted a butchery department. Gary Graham, who ran errands to the Co-op for his grandmother in the 1940s, can still remember her 'divi' number – 23853 – can you remember your mother's or grandmother's? In the 1990s the original home of the Co-op housed Bangor Auctions. Today it serves as an art gallery, and Gray's Hill is known as Bangor's antiques quarter.

Photographer:
Adam Bell

Princetown Road

Princetown Road, Bangor.

Posted 17 August 1911
*Publisher: Eason & Son Ltd,
Dublin & Belfast*

Princetown Road lies along the eastern edge of what was once known as 'Great Forte Hill'. Home to some of Bangor's finest villas, including Seacourt, Glenbank and Augustaville, Princetown Road follows the line of the coast to Wilson's Point, where it joins Maxwell Road. The picturesque terrace with deep-eaved dormers and frilly bargeboards is Ardmore Cottages, built about 1880. The stone built building in the far distance, with its gable to the road, served as the stables for no 56, one half of the two storey semi-villa known as Martello. It was from this house in 1905 that a servant girl threw herself out of a second storey window. Although the unfortunate girl was apparently uninjured, she "was certified to be a dangerous lunatic" on account of a religious mania, and consigned to the Down District Lunatic Asylum.

Photographer:
Gerry Coe

Princetown Terrace, Mount Royal, Mount Pleasant, Pickie Terrace and Lorelei are all accessed by lanes off Princetown Road. The lanes leading to Mount Royal and Mount Pleasant can be seen in this view, either side of Ardmore Cottages. In the early 1960s Mrs Eccles of Chatsworth House, 2 Princetown Terrace, offered visitors to her guest house "modern comforts" and a "liberal and varied menu" for £7 7s per week (high season). Matching Mrs Eccles' price, Mrs E Hambly of Norlyn House, Mount Royal, hoped to tempt holidaymakers with her "home baking" and the fact that there was a television on the premises. For an extra 13 shillings, the Misses Abbott at Sharon Guest House, 5 Pickie Terrace, guaranteed "personal supervision" and "superior accommodation" including "H & C in bedrooms" and beds with "interior springs". Guest houses on the same terraces today offer "satellite TV", "internet access" and "family rooms" as inducements.

Pickie Terrace and Lorelei

The Pickie Rock Hotel Bangor Co. Down.

Posted 19 July 1911
Publisher: Lawrence, Dublin

Overlooking Bangor Bay, Pickie Terrace (left) and Lorelei (right) were built in the last decades of the nineteenth century. Pickie Rock Hotel occupied nos 1–3 Pickie Terrace, including the distinctive four storey square Italianate tower seen on the side of no 1. Lorelei was built in stages, nos 3 and 4 coming about a decade before nos 1, 2, 5 and 6. Directly below Pickie Terrace was the Gentlemen's Bathing Place, as it was known at the time of this postcard, latterly becoming Pickie Pool.

Sent by Meg McManus to her mother at 3 Edgar Street, Belfast, the message reads, "Dear mother. Arrived here safe. Aunt Aggie met me at the station. Having a good time, I am going over to Newtownards on Thursday or Friday. I will be home on Saturday. I suppose you are glad to get rid of me. I was bathing this morning and it was great. Tell father to be good, also James. Love from Meg x".

Photographer:
Viv Beck

Bangor Collegiate School purchased the former Pickie Rock Hotel in 1919. The school had been established about 1880 as a private school for girls, and was located at Gray's Hill before the move to Pickie Terrace. As the school expanded, the preparatory department moved in 1950 to Avoca, a large house on Princetown Road, and in 1957 Bangor Collegiate amalgamated with Glenlola School. Lorelei was known as the home of the Tedworth Hotel for many years. An early advertisement from 1960 promoted it as the "Tedworth Christian Guest House" run by Mr and Mrs Baxter. In 1960 the Tedworth occupied nos 4 and 5, but it was later to take over most of the terrace. In 1999 Lorelei was demolished, except for the façade, which was retained and incorporated into the new apartment block. Nos 1–3 Pickie Terrace have also since been rebuilt. The area in the foreground is the recently renovated Pickie Fun Park, which now boasts a new maritime themed mini golf course and water play area in addition to the ever popular Pickie Puffer miniature train and swan pedaloes.

Pickie Pool

Bangor showing Pickie Pool, Co. Down, N.I.

Photo : E. Nägele, John Hinde Studios.

Unposted, about 1965
Publisher: John Hinde Ltd
Photographer: Edmund Nägele

Pickie Rock was a popular spot for bathing as early as the 1860s, when a rudimentary bathing shelter was erected there by Mr McFall, proprietor of the Royal Hotel. By the 1880s it had increased its reputation as a "favourite resort of gentlemen bathers" and a "small concrete and stone dressing house" was erected by RE Ward. The building seen in this view is the new Pickie Pool which was opened in 1931. The pool itself was 100 feet square, ranging from 2 ½ to 15 feet deep, with a 33 foot diving board, water chutes, and springboards into the open sea. It was promoted as the largest and best equipped open air pool in Ireland, with tiered seating for 1,500 spectators, a "well-equipped café" which served warming cups of Bovril and "dressing boxes … heated in chilly weather by means of hot-water pipes". It was the venue for the All Ireland National Swimming and Diving Championships as well as playing host to regular Saturday evening galas organised by Bangor Amateur Swimming Club. In 1957 admission for adult bathers was 1/-, children and spectators 6d. In addition to the galas and championships that year, legendary long distance swimmer Jack McClelland undertook an "all-night swim" on 19 July.

Photographer:
David Roberts

Many look back with fondness to youthful summers spent at Pickie Pool for which, at its height, 1,000 tickets a day were issued. Andy Johnston was the superintendant for many years, teaching hundreds of youngsters how to swim using his famous technique of dragging them through the water on the end of a rope! Karen Cooley recalls, "As you went through the turnstile the pool and sea temperatures were written in chalk on a blackboard, the average temperature for the pool being about 64 degrees and the sea perhaps 54–58 degrees". To the left of the pool, anchored to the sea bed was a raft. Karen also remembers that "the boys used to stand on your fingers as the girls tried to climb on board the raft". To the right of the pool was a shallow paddling area for young children, and along the front of the building were shelters, a convenient spot from which to watch the American square dancing which drew large crowds in the 1950s. By the 1980s, the comfort and convenience of Bangor Castle Leisure Centre with its indoor heated pool heralded the end of Pickie, and in its last month of operation in 1986 it was used by fewer than 800 people.

The Amphitheatre, Marine Gardens

The Amphitheatre, Bangor, Co. Down

Posted 11 October 1922
Publisher: Valentine, Dublin

Beyond Pickie, the Amphitheatre was the location of the Ladies Bathing Place, part of which is glimpsed here at bottom right. Featuring rocky outcrops and tastefully arranged plantations of shrubbery and hardy trees, around and above which wound interlacing footways dotted with benches, the Amphitheatre was a much enjoyed part of Marine Gardens. In 1912 it was the site of an anti Home Rule rally, when around 5,000 people packed into the space. The small structure with the hipped roof is a timber pavilion, no doubt appreciated as a place of refuge for those caught out by a rainstorm. In the distance on the right is Glenbank, one of the finest of Bangor's 'big houses'. Sent to Miss E Davidson c/o Mrs Christie of Hatfield Street off Belfast's Ormeau Road, the message on this postcard reads, "Just a card to ask how you are getting along. I hope you are not feeling too lonely and that mother is keeping well! I am looking forward to getting word by tomorrow. With kind regards, Etta".

Photographer:
Gerry Coe

The changing rooms for the Ladies Bathing Place were removed following the Second World War. Innisfail, the large house seen at left in the postcard view, has been considerably altered since it was built about 1906. Glenbank, the grand house once lived in by Dean Edward Maguire, first Rector of St Comgall's Parish Church, also remains in its prominent position looking out to sea, although a century's growth of trees and shrubs has now largely shielded both houses from view. In 1903, the year Dean Maguire moved into Glenbank, his son Frederick married into the Davidson family of nearby Seacourt, the most palatial house on Princetown Road. Both Glenbank and Seacourt have since been divided into apartments and their grounds built upon.

Ladies Bathing Place, Skippingstone

LADIES BATHING PLACE, BANGOR.

Unposted, about 1910
*Publisher: Eason & Son Ltd,
Dublin & Belfast*

The Ladies Bathing Place was situated at the Marine Gardens Amphitheatre, about 250 yards to the west of the Gentlemen's Bathing Place, later Pickie Pool. Known as Skippingstone, the pool took its name from the "deposit of smooth stones" found in the area. In order to get this image, the photographer, WA Green, must surely have broken one of Bangor Urban District Council's bye-laws, which restricted the nearest approach of any male to 100 yards! The *Official Guide to Bangor* for 1935 states that Skippingstone was provided with a "tidal pond (one foot to six feet gradient), and also spring boards, from which the 'sea nymphs' can indulge in 'headers' into the open sea". Note the group of young men gathered at the end of the wall at right, taking a keen interest in the sea nymphs!

Photographer:
Adam Bell

Mixed bathing was introduced at Pickie in 1916, not however without considerable debate on the morality of such a daring move! Skippingstone remained a female only preserve, reserved for ladies and very young children. The 1935 *Guide* contrasts the "hilarious merriment of the bathers at Pickie" with the "more dignified grace at Skippingstone". By 1940 it was open in July and August only, and it presumably closed soon after, as no mention is made of it in the post-war guides. Although the accompanying buildings providing changing facilities have now gone, part of the concrete pool enclosure can still be seen. The bandstand, located from 1915 on a grassy mound to the right of the image has now found a new home in Bangor Castle Walled Garden.

Wilson's Point

Pickie from the Glen, Bangor, Co. Down.

Unposted, about 1925
*Publisher: Eason & Son Ltd,
Dublin & Belfast*

This view shows the cove at Wilson's Point, with the castellated boundary wall of Seacourt in the distance. Foster Connor, a Belfast linen merchant, built Seacourt about 1865. In 1895 Samuel Davidson, founder of Belfast's Sirocco Works, purchased the house and its 18 acres of grounds for £5,000. A keen yachtsman, Davidson entertained fellow Royal Ulster Yacht Club member Sir Thomas Lipton on his visits to Bangor, and he had a stone tower built on the edge of his property, from which to watch the yacht racing. Seacourt even had its own private bathing box, which can be seen in the middle distance at left. The women in the foreground are probably on their way to Strickland's Glen, described in the 1938 *Official Guide* as "a delightfully picturesque rural retreat, much in favour with picknickers (sic) and excursionists". Nestled in the leafy glen was an establishment called The Bungalow where tea and refreshments could be had until the 1940s.

As popular with walkers today as it was 90 years ago, the coastal path is practically unaltered, apart from the removal of the steps visible in the foreground opposite. Seacourt was purchased in 1972 by Down County Education Committee and converted into a Teachers' Centre, then in 1989 the house and its grounds were again sold, this time seeing the conversion of the house into apartments and the development of its grounds. If the photographer of the 1920s view had turned around, high above on the left would have stood Thalassa, another grand house surrounded by extensive grounds, sadly demolished in 2007.

Homes of Rest, Downshire Road

Homes of Rest Bangor Co. Down.

Posted 23 August 1908
Publisher: Lawrence, Dublin

Situated on a commanding site at the bottom of Downshire Road overlooking Smelt Mill Bay and Belfast Lough are the Homes of Rest, which were built over a period of ten years from 1898. Financed by a philanthropist named Vance, the Homes provided bed, board and healthy surroundings to the needy, including "white-faced little mortals fading in sultry back streets". On the far left is the Canon Stewart Home of Rest for Men & Lads and at far right is the Mrs Foster Green Home for Mothers & Children. The house at centre was erected in memory of Lydia Montgomery Stewart and was known as the Mrs Stewart Home for Cripples. Sent to Miss M Dempster of Paisley in August 1904, the message on this card simply reads, "Dear Mysie. This is not where we are staying. Yours, Jenny".

Photographer:
Deborah Carvill

At their height the Homes of Rest, including another at the foot of Brompton Road – the Girls' Home – provided an estimated 7,000 Belfast people annually with a week's holiday by the sea. While Jenny was at pains to point out that she was not actually staying at the Homes, the author also has cards in his collection which were sent by those who were. Margaret Fowler wrote to her friend Miss Irvine from the Girls' Home in 1907, "I am feeling a great deal better & take my food much better" while Sammy Patterson wrote from the Canon Stewart Home in 1921, advising his mother that the weather was not so good, and that "you will have to square up Mrs Hogg this week yourself". Today the Stewart Memorial Nursing Unit and self contained apartments form Stricklands Care Village administered by the Northern Ireland Institute for the Disabled, providing care and support for people with disabilities.

The Long Hole looking east

Clifden Bangor, Co. Down.

Unposted, about 1905–1907
Publisher: Lawrence, Dublin

The Long Hole, or the Big Hole as it was often commonly called, is a picturesque creek at the western end of Seacliff Road, which for generations has provided shelter for small boats. Although its origins are uncertain, it may have been a naturally occurring, but shallow, harbour, which was enlarged by quarrying in about 1815. Tradition has it that the excavated stone was used to build the Bangor Castle demesne wall, while another school of thought suggests that it may have been used in the construction of an early breakwater. Although mainly the preserve of small fishing and pleasure boats, the Long Hole was also where the Belfast-Bangor paddle steamers *Erin* and *Bangor Castle* were moored during the winter months of the 1880s. Overlooking the Long Hole and with uninterrupted sea views are many fine late Victorian terraces and villas.

Photographer:
Adam Bell

Little altered in the course of a century, the Long Hole is today just as picturesque. One difference to note is the surfacing of the rocks on the seaward side, undertaken to improve access in the 1950s. Although not visible in the postcard view opposite, 'Vote for Ferguson' was at some point daubed in large capital letters on the landward side of the rocks, and is visible in postcard views dating from about 1910 through to the 1930s. Development along Seacliff Road has been almost exclusively on the inland side, but there are a few exceptions. Seacliff, built about 1780, is a two storey L-shaped block of houses built out on the rocks, visible in the distance at far left. At one time called Saltpans, salt making was formerly carried on there. With its back to the water, its first occupants clearly appreciated shelter from the cruel sea over the picturesque views so prized by the late Victorian developers.

The slipway, Seacliff Road

No. 34 SEACLIFF ROAD, BANGOR, CO. DOWN.

Unposted, about 1914
Publisher: Hurst & Co, Belfast

In this view we get a closer look at some of the fine terraces that line Seacliff Road. Seen jutting out onto the rocky foreshore at far left, Seacliff was built in the late eighteenth century. It stood alone until Clifton Terrace was built to its right about 1857. In the following decades Bangor was developed as a summer resort. The dirt track skirting along the coast to Ballyholme became Seacliff Road and by the closing years of the century most of the buildings seen in this view had been erected. This postcard was written by 'Annie' to her cousin Fred Robinson, although it was not posted. Annie has marked with a cross where she has taken up residence for the summer, and indicated with two crosses where her Aunt Mary was residing. She writes that the family have taken the same house "this past two years" and that it is "great value".

Photographer:
Bobby Peacock

Were it not for the men with straw boaters and ladies with long dresses, the view opposite could almost have been taken today. On close inspection of the postcard image, the buildings at far right display signs which read 'Clifton Café' and 'American Studio'. The Clifton Café was run by Mrs Mary Wylie at nos 58–60 Seacliff Road and the proprietor of the American Studio at no 62, listed as a "shed" in contemporary directories, was Rowland Gledhill. In 1914 Bangor had four photographers, three of which operated their businesses from Seacliff Road. Charles Haig specialised in "midget photographs" at just "6d per dozen" at his studio on the corner of Ward Avenue and Seacliff Road, while William Abernethy boasted that his photographic studio at 2 Gray's Hill was "By Royal Appointment to Her Majesty the late Queen Victoria", no doubt appealing to a middle class clientele.

Seacliff Road and the Long Hole looking west

Bangor Co.Down.

Posted 17 April 1906
Publisher: W Lawrence, Dublin

This is an uncommon view, as the majority of postcards show the Long Hole looking from the other end. Although most of the fine houses along this stretch of Seacliff Road had by now been built, the site of Knightsbridge, a terrace of three storey houses erected about 1905 just beyond 'Ailsa Terrace' (seen in the foreground at left) is vacant. Visible beyond the Long Hole is the 'New Pier', constructed in 1895. Overlooking the pier and built at about the same time was Redcliffe, the three storey red brick home of Dr RL Moore, which is today the Salty Dog Hotel & Bistro. Redcliffe replaced a small whitewashed cottage, known after its occupant as Sally Beattie's Cottage. Addressed to Miss A Minnis of 150 Woodstock Road, Belfast, the sender of this postcard writes, "Hoping you are enjoying your Easter Holidays. Yours, Ciss".

Both images were taken from the flight of steps leading up to no 88 Seacliff Road, built about 1885. At first glance, it would seem that the photographer of the postcard view, employed by the studio of William Lawrence, captured an Irish jaunting car ambling along Seacliff Road. A closer look reveals that while there are two passengers, sitting on opposite sides of the carriage, there is no driver! Perhaps the photographer and his assistant were brought here on the jaunting car. Edwardian photographers rarely missed an opportunity to arrange a few bystanders or orchestrate an interesting scene in the foreground, so it is quite likely that the photographer asked his assistant and the driver to pose while he photographed the scene.

Royal Ulster Yacht Club

Royal Ulster Yacht Club (Co. Down).   Valentine's Series

Posted 27 April 1907
Publisher: Valentine, Dublin

The Ulster Yacht Club was founded by Lord Dufferin in 1866. Under Dufferin's energetic commodoreship, the club received a Royal Charter in 1870. By the 1890s the two-day RUYC regatta was attracting "all the big yachts" of the British Isles and beyond including, in 1896, the Prince of Wales' yacht *Britannia* and *Meteor,* which was sailed by the German Emperor Wilhelm II. Charles Milligan recalled the RUYC regattas of this time, when "in the evening you could see a forest of masts in Bangor Bay and also five or six big steam yachts".

The club's most famous member was the grocery magnate Sir Thomas Lipton, whose humble upbringing in the slums of Glasgow debarred him from membership of the exclusive Royal Yacht Squadron at Cowes. Lipton was to launch five challenges for the America's Cup from the RUYC between 1898 and 1929, in fact the sender of this postcard informed the recipient, Miss Nellie Tyler of Liverpool, that "the RUYC on other side is Lipton's headquarters".

Photographer:
Gerry Coe

The attractive arts and crafts clubhouse, designed by RUYC member and architect Vincent Craig, was opened in 1899. Externally, a veranda and front porch have since been added, but the interior retains much of its original late Victorian splendour, including an elaborate staircase carved with shipping and foliate designs. The villa to the right of the clubhouse in the view opposite was named Ardmara. Built about 1860, it was one of Bangor's finest early villas. At six o'clock one morning in February 1999, the residents of Clifton Road were awakened by the sound of Ardmara being razed to the ground. The

timing and haste of the operation, not to say anything of the shocking action itself, stunned many. In fact the building was even demolished while its electricity supply was still live, and the rubble was set on fire. Nearby Ward Villas, built in 1855, also succumbed to the same fate. In 2000 the Ulster Architectural Heritage Society commented that "North Down, and Bangor in particular, seems to have caught a severe case of developer-itis. No sooner is a moderately large patch of back garden spotted or a large house with any surrounding land put on the market than the disease strikes".

Ballyholme Bay from Seaforth Road

Posted 23 July 1904
Publisher: Unknown

At the turn of the twentieth century the two and three storey terraces of Ballyholme Esplanade were newly built, mostly as summer or seaside houses for Belfast's well-to-do. However, much of Ballyholme was still undeveloped, being either common land or farmland. The extension of Seacliff Road past Luke's Point and along to Ballyholme Road was another recent development of the time. The ornate iron gates in the foreground at right belong to Ardmore, a substantial villa used from 1897 to 1900 as Dr Connolly's Intermediate School, forerunner of the present Bangor Grammar. Sent by 'Mary' to Miss Byrne of 9 Northfield, Killaughey Road, Donaghadee, the message on this card reads, "My dear M, I was very sorry that you couldn't come. We had such fun. We were all singing and I did the cake walk. Lizzie and Cassie were both down". Originating in America, the 'cake walk' was a popular ragtime dance craze, characterised by "prancing steps".

Photographer:
Gerry Coe

Whereas Ballyholme Bay could be seen clearly in the postcard view opposite, the present day vista is very different, affording just a glimpse of Belfast Terrace (nos 12–21 Ballyholme Esplanade). Seaforth Road links Ward Avenue with Seacliff Road and was laid out about 1890. The one and a half storey house at far left in the postcard view was replaced in the 1990s, however a similar house built alongside, soon after the postcard image was taken, remains today. Just visible on the horizon of the Edwardian view is Ballyholme Windmill, which dominated the green fields of Ballyholme and Ballymagee from its construction about 1780 until it was gutted by fire in 1922. Thereafter it was adapted for use as a dwelling, minus its cap and sails, and is today surrounded by semi-detached houses built in the 1920s and 1930s.

Caproni's Ballroom and Café

RECREATION GROUNDS, BALLYHOLME BAY, BANGOR   R 4666

Unposted, photographed 1955
Publisher: Valentine & Sons Ltd

Enrico Caproni, originally from Barga in the Tuscany region of Italy, arrived in Bangor in 1900. His "world famed ice cream" proved a hit with locals and visitors alike, and business boomed. Following on from the opening of his ice cream emporium on Queen's Parade, Caproni's Palais de Danse and Mirimar Café opened at Ballyholme in 1925. It soon gained a reputation as Bangor's premier dancehall, and people would come from far and wide for the best bands of the day.

Inside was a famous sign which read, "Through these doors, from time to time, pass some of the most beautiful women in the world". Strict rules were enforced at 'Caps'; no alcohol was to be drunk on the premises and commissionaires refused entry to those whose dress or appearance was not deemed appropriate. At the stroke of midnight the national anthem would be played, signalling that dancing was over for another night.

When Caproni's closed in 1977 it was the end of an era for Bangor. The famous building with its sprung dance floor and white marble staircase was eventually demolished in 1983, to be replaced by a block of flats. In the foreground, the tennis courts and putting green remain popular attractions. It was in 1915 that the Urban District Council acquired the Clifton Recreation Grounds, thereafter known as Kingsland. Up to that point, the land had been used as playing fields for Dr Connolly's Intermediate School as well as hosting summer amusements including circuses, funfairs and even, until it was destroyed in the 'big wind' of 1894, a switchback railway. Visible at the foreshore in the view opposite, the modest facilities belonging to Ballyholme Yacht Club (est 1900) have since been replaced by a more commodious clubhouse, complete with observation lounge and bar. The original 'dainty' clubhouse, used before the First World War, is still in use today as the Kingsland pavilion.

Ballyholme Bay looking east

ESPLANADE, BALLYHOLME, BANGOR, CO. DOWN.   R.343

Unposted, photographed 1936
Publisher: Valentine & Sons Ltd

This postcard shows just how popular Ballyholme was in the mid decades of the last century. In a scene typical of the time, we see couples out for a stroll, mothers with children and babies in perambulators, and further along, hundreds of holidaymakers enjoying themselves on the sands. In the summer months, coach loads of day-trippers would descend upon Ballyholme, direct from Belfast. "You knew they had been afterwards!" recalls Terry Swanston, who lived at 56

Ballyholme Road in the 1960s. They came for Ballyholme's "glorious bay", described in the 1938 *Official Guide to Bangor* as "so often coupled with Naples for beauty". The guide also said of beach bathing at Ballyholme, "Dressing boxes are available. With the erection of new cloakroom and the introduction of an hygienic clothes hanger system, the dressing accommodation is increased five fold, and irksome waits for boxes are now eliminated".

Today the "glorious bay" is just as much of an asset to the Borough, although the availability of affordable foreign holidays from the later twentieth century has meant that most people, given the chance, prefer to visit the actual bay of Naples over its near rival at Ballyholme! The bungalow with the attractive leaded windows, visible on the right in both images, was built about 1910. In the late 1940s, while repairing the lead flashing on the roof of this bungalow, Belfast plumber Ted Petherick slipped and fell off, landing in the garden below. The lady of the house rushed out with a glass of whiskey, thinking to settle poor Ted's nerves, but she was too generous in her measure and, after half a tumbler of the spirit, he wasn't fit to continue working on the roof that day! A bit further along from this bungalow, the three storey red brick terrace at the end of Ballyholme Road, on the seaward side, was formerly the Seabreeze Café, proffering day-trippers "Teas, coffees, minerals & ices".

Ballyholme Park

Ballyholme Park, Bangor, Co. Down.

Posted about 1907
*Publisher: James Conolly,
Scrabo House, Bangor*

Well known for many years as the Ballyholme Hotel, the three storey terrace overlooking the bay at centre was built about 1890. Between 1901 and 1905 it was occupied by Dr Connolly's Intermediate School, which moved in 1906 to new buildings on College Avenue and was thereafter known as Bangor Grammar. Although not franked, this postcard probably dates to about 1907 or shortly after, when the Urban District Council acquired the land at left and laid out Ballyholme Park. Without doubt the best message I have come across on a postcard, the lady author, identified only as 'A.S.M.' writes, "How are you all? Everything is so very quiet here. In fact there seems to be no life left in Bangor. Young men seem all to have gone & what is left is either dying or getting married". Clearly, the Bangor season had come to an end and A.S.M.'s prospects of finding an eligible bachelor were slipping away! The card was sent to Miss A Sewell of Detroit, Michigan.

At first glance you could be forgiven for thinking that the terrace formerly occupied by the Ballyholme Hotel has stood untouched, looking majestically over the bay since it was built about 1890. But look at bit closer and you will discover that it has gained an extra storey! In August 2000 the terrace was all but demolished, apart from the ground floor façade, from which arose a new apartment block, the design of which mimics the original building. To its right is now a nursing home, but for much of the twentieth century this was the site of the Ballyholme boatyard, founded by Mr Lovett and later operated by Mr Slater originally of Workman & Clark. The brown brick apartments further along were built on the site of Caproni's ballroom.

Ballyholme Esplanade looking east

Ballyholme, Bangor, Co. Down

Posted 7 August 1916
Publisher: Valentine, Dublin
Retailer: William Dunn, 26, 28
& 30 Main Street, Bangor

Before consecutive numbering of houses was commonplace, groups of houses or 'Terraces' were often given names. In fact the *Spectator Year Book and Directory* for 1918 contained 11 pages headed 'Names of Villas and Terraces in Bangor'. Of the 82 Terraces listed in 1918, six were on Ballyholme Esplanade. At far right in the view above is Ballyholme Terrace, followed by St Helier's, Belfast, Balfour, Victoria and Bayview Terraces. St Helier's Terrace is the pair of two and a half storey houses on the corner of Godfrey Avenue. When St Helier's was being painted its unfortunate builder, John Jamison, fell down the bank while walking backwards to inspect the job! In the foreground, facing Waverley Drive, is the stone retaining wall of 'Folly Bridge' which originally crossed a stream, now culverted underground. Sent to Miss M Fitzpatrick at the Royal Victoria Hospital Belfast, 'Norah' wrote, "Having very nice weather, and am feeling much better".

Photographer:
Bobby Peacock

Much of the land at Ballyholme was owned by two farmers, Andy Lamont and his brother John. John lived in a whitewashed cottage near Waverley Drive until his death in 1915. As a boy in the late 1880s and 1890s, Charles Milligan lived with his family at Royal Terrace in Belfast, but they spent the summer months at Hamilton Villas, adjoining Dufferin Villas to the east of Ballyholme Bay. Charles recalled that "one half of Ballyholme, and all the houses in Dufferin Villas would be locked up in the winter". A few doors up from the Milligans on Royal Terrace were two old ladies who, according to Charles, had "seen better days and were, so to speak, trying to keep up with the Joneses. In due course the blinds would come down and the house would be locked up in July, and re-opened in August". The ladies were, however, discovered to be living at home in the back premises, "on the pretence of being away on holiday".

Ballyholme Bay looking west

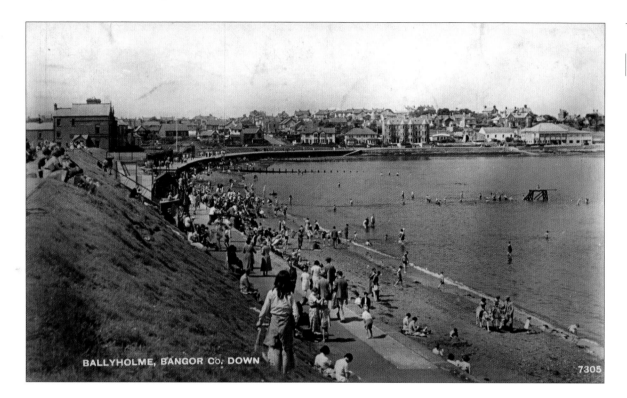

BALLYHOLME, BANGOR Co. DOWN

7305

Posted 19 August 1948
*Publisher: Scholastic
Production Co, Belfast*

The *Official Guide to Bangor* for 1940 says of bathing at Ballyholme, "Ballyholme sands extend for some two miles and provide safe bathing at all stages of the tide. Here gay bathing parties laze away the hot afternoons, children in sun suits paddle or play in perfect safety, whilst parents relax in deck chairs, their cares forgotten. Dressing boxes are available at moderate cost and there are two spring-boards". Sent to 'Jeannie' at 24 Maymount Street, Woodstock Road, Belfast,

'Minnie' writes, "I thought you would have come to Bangor one day this week. The weather hasn't been too bad". Minnie was staying at 7 Beatrice Avenue while in Bangor. Alex Jamison, Bangor's last town crier, lived at 5 Beatrice Avenue until his death in 1945. Although a painter by trade, Alex would go round the town ringing a bell to announce auctions and other events of general interest.

Bathing boxes were installed at Ballyholme in 1914 to provide changing facilities for the increasing number of sea bathers. A few years later, in July 1918, it is amusing to record a report in the *County Down Spectator*, that "In order to discourage persons bathing in 'birthday' costumes at Ballyholme, it was resolved that Sergeant Johnston be asked to permit a constable in plain clothes to patrol the district". Hilary Davis remembers the roof of Ballyholme's bathing boxes as being a good place from which to sunbathe in the 1950s. It also happened, Hilary recalls, to be a good vantage point for another popular pastime – "watching the boys"! Today the bathing boxes, diving boards and raft, well used in Bangor's heyday as a summer resort, have since been removed.

Ballyholme Esplanade looking west

BALLYHOLME NEAR BANGOR, CO. DOWN.

Posted 11 September 1907
Publisher: Frederick Hartmann

In 1867 Ballyholme Bay was described as "the very spot for civilised bathing – but quite neglected". All that was to change, for by the late 1890s the long promenade, with steps to the beach below and Ballyholme Esplanade above, had been constructed. At far left is Balfour Terrace, to the left of which originally stood farmer John 'Jockey' Hamilton's thatched cottage with its gable to the sea. Hamilton's farm was the site of Ballyholme Showgrounds, where circuses were staged. Sisters Frances and Natalie Murphy recall going to see the circus at Ballyholme in the late 1920s, an abiding memory of which was seeing a black man swallowing a sword and dancing on hot coals. Sent to Mr S Heaney at 36 St Ives Gardens, Stranmillis Road, Belfast, the message reads, "30 Gray's Hill, Bangor. Down here since Saty. Enjoying our holidays splendidly. Am delighted with Bangor. Weather is lovely, not a drop of rain. Kind regards, L.H."

Photographer:
Viv Beck

As well as a venue for staging circuses, the Showgrounds was also home to Bangor Football Club, before it moved to Clandeboye Park in 1934. Soon after, Sandringham Drive was built on the site, and the pair of two storey pebbledashed semis, seen here at far left, replaced 'Jockey' Hamilton's farmhouse. In addition to the pleasures of sea bathing at Ballyholme's "glorious bay", the beach was also the occasional location for thrilling spectacles, such as the flying display in June 1914 by the French aviator Henri Salmet. Hundreds of awestruck spectators gathered to watch Salmet's "skill and daring" as "the machine rose like a bird on the wing and circled Ballyholme Bay". Another impressive spectacle occurred during the Second World War at the eastern stretch of Ballyholme Bay where, shortly before D Day, "The crews of some of the tank loading craft were trained" and there was a "full scale embarkation exercise".

BANGOR THEN AND NOW

Acknowledgements

This book would not have been possible without the assistance of Bangor & North Down Camera Club (BNDCC), members of which gave up their time to take many of the present day views. Particular thanks are due to BNDCC President Gerry Coe and club members Deborah Carvill, May Carvill, Henry Doggart, Helen Fettus, Angus Gardiner, Michael Graham, Shirley Graham, Alan Hartley, Ali Martin, Kevin Neupert, Bobby Peacock, David Roberts, Angela Shannon, Nigel Snell, Jack Thompson and Harry Watson, with additional photography by Viv Beck, Karl Grierson and the author.

I am indebted to Sandra Millsopp, Marcus Patton and Ian Wilson for their valuable insights, comments and support, and to those who shared their memories with me, including Cherie Bell, Seamus Bowler, Raymond Brown, Peter Clark, Karen Cooley, Roger Corry, Hilary Davis, Gary Graham, Margaret Graham, Claire Gray, Sheila Hoey, Tom Hoey, Jack McCloskey, Lloyd Morgan, Frances Murphy, Natalie Murphy, Paul Murray, Carolyn Powell, Hazel Ringland, Dorothy Swanston and Terry Swanston.

Thanks also go to Clandeboye Estate, Cathy Cree (North Down YMCA), Paul Donegan, Terry Eakin, Dorothy Fleet, Maud Hamill (Abbey Historical Society), Gwen McCullough, John Miskimmon (Northern Ireland Institute for the Disabled), John Stenhouse and E Williams for their kind assistance.

The author is grateful for permission to reproduce the images on p56 and p86, which are © John Hinde Ltd.

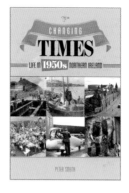
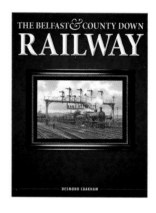
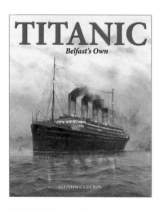
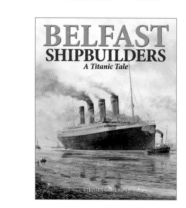
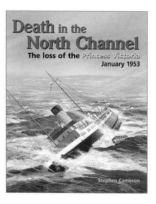
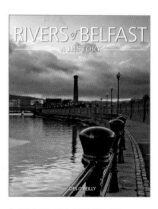